A LETTER TO TIA

GRIEF. GRIEVING. THE LOVE, PAIN AND LOSS OF A FRIEND

BY DON LANDY

ISBN-10: 1482590654

ISBN-13: 9781482590654

Library of Congress Control Number: 2013903535
CreateSpace Independent Publishing Platform
North Charleston, South Carolina

Printed by CreateSpace
Cover photos by C. Landy and Heidimarie

Dedicated to Kimberly Goodrich, DVM, Heidi Ward DVM, and anyone who has loved or lost a special friend.

Table of Contents

CHAPTER 1
YOU CAN'T RUN AWAY FROM BAD NEWS

You can't run away from bad news: grief and grieving won't allow it!

On April 7, 2011, I could feel the tears coming as I listened to your veterinary surgeon, Dr. Kimberly Goodrich, explain the results of the four biopsies taken after she repaired your flipped stomach.

Three days had passed since your surgery, a very long three days, and although we were anxious to learn the results of the biopsy readings, Mom and I had our fingers crossed and were holding our breaths, hoping against hope they would come back negative. It was one of those times when you wanted the information and yet you weren't really sure you wanted to hear it.

"Tia has cancer. The prognosis is six to eight months, and a 10 percent chance of survival."

My heart stopped.

There was more, but the rest didn't really matter. What could we ask, what could we say? Our worst nightmare had become a reality—cancer. We thanked the doctor for the news.

The first thing that came to mind after the immediate shock was "This can't be happening, not again." But it was. I fought to hold back the tears that had already begun to flow, took a couple of deep breaths, and tried to get my head around what I'd just heard.

It didn't work. A voice was shouting *No!* over and over again. It was me, my subconscious mind in overdrive.

I stood stone silent, alone in the darkness of my thoughts. I turned away from Mom, hoping to hide the tears washing over me. My shoulders were beginning to quiver. I felt as though my mind and body were being turned inside out.

The voice was back, reminding me that we had been here once before as it asked, *What did you learn the first time?*

That I needed to think, plan, and get control of my emotions before I could begin to move forward. Easier said than done when you feel as though your feet are nailed to the floor!

You had just turned four, four—four years old! A few days ago you were a happy-go-lucky child celebrating a birthday and the arrival of some new toys, right?

Wrong!

We just didn't know it. Cancer sneaks up on you when you least expect it and before you know it.

That voice was right; I had been here before, and the outcome had broken my heart.

Who says that life is fair?

And how was your day?

Not long ago I spent the better part of eleven years praying for miracles. Your sister, Sabrina, faced one physical problem after another. I never loved so hard and cried so much, all the while asking God for help. And then, just shy of her eleventh birthday, cancer took her away from us.

I was torn when I should have been grateful. After all, she had been with us far longer than her veterinarians expected, but at that moment all I could ask was, "Why, *why* couldn't He have found an easier way to bring her home?"

Some people dream about life and love, but never find it. I'm not talking about the ho-hum, nine-to-five, two-cars, two-kids, and house-with-a-white-picket-fence kind of love. I'm talking about the real thing. A life that challenges you mentally and physically—one in which at times you hear yourself screaming *No-o-o-o, this can't be happening!* The type of challenge that leaves you telling yourself over and over again, *I won't give in, I won't give up!*

My mind was ready, though unwilling, to process and accept the news that like Sabrina, you had inoperable cancer. I was down on my knees—mentally, as I challenged God's decision—demanding answers.

It seemed like only yesterday that I'd received similar news, but in truth it had been nearly five years.

Sabrina had spent a good part of her life rehabbing from one surgery after another as she fought to walk, and then run again, before cancer ravaged her body.

Suddenly I was faced with keeping a promise I had made to her and myself to never allow her to be in pain. I could not, *would not* stand by and watch her body shrink before my eyes just so that I might have her with me for a few additional weeks or months.

Well, today was a real stinker.

You have cancer!

The prognosis—death!

I don't know why, but the words *boundaries and limitations* and *They are just dogs, treat them that way* flashed through my mind once again. Those were the words I had heard repeated several times by dog trainers. And once again, those words seemed obscene.

Five years earlier I had never thought about grief and grieving, didn't know what they were, much less how I would know when I faced them. Then, along came a total stranger named Mitch. I had placed a call to a pet loss grief counseling hotline. I had no idea what to expect. I was hurting, searching, reaching out for help and understanding.

Mitch listened patiently as I poured my heart out over the telephone.

How was I supposed to feel when I was confronted with the excruciating pain of what turned out to be grieving?

Feelings! What feelings? I was a mental and physical train wreck. I was experiencing the kind of pain that individuals, never having loved a dog or a cat, would have difficulty wrapping their minds around.

How do you respond? Do you stand by and watch cancer tear a friend or loved one apart before your eyes?

I had watched what it had done to friends. It wasn't pretty, and I wanted no part of it for you, my beautiful little girl—you deserved better!

Looking back, I had never wanted a dog or cat, yet I have never forgotten the first time I felt the pain of loss nearly thirty years ago. It was over a cat. His name was Charlie Brown. He was a sleek chestnut Oriental Shorthair. I had picked Charlie as I watched your mom deliver a new litter of kittens. From the moment of birth he was mine!

Did I fail to mention that the love of my life, your mom, bred show cats for many years?

Charlie wasn't with us very long, but then, love can't be measured in time!

Grief! At the time all I knew was I was crying my heart out and had no idea why.

The tears began to flow the minute I learned that Charlie needed heart surgery. I was several hundred miles from home at the time, in a business meeting, and yet, when I heard Mom explain Charlie's condition I didn't hesitate to tell her, "Do whatever it takes to save him!"

I had been offered an empty office to take an emergency call and when I hung up the phone the tears were coming hard and fast. I sat in that office for a few minutes in an effort to compose myself and then went back into the meeting. Staying on an even keel wasn't easy.

As it turned out, Charlie's little heart was unable to withstand the surgery and upon learning his fate, I found myself shedding tears on the ride to the airport and during the return flight home.

Grieving? I was engulfed in it, I guess. My tears didn't stop when I walked in to the house.

Tears don't just turn themselves off. I cried off and on for months after his passing. Believe it or not, even now if I sit down and reread the stories I wrote to myself after he died, about the time we shared together, the tears start all over again.

Charlie was small, but he had the heart of a lion. He wasn't much to look at as a kitten, but suddenly he blossomed as an adult.

His proportions, once a laughingstock, were just right. If you remember your fairy tales, Charlie was the frog that became a prince. He and I took a lot of abuse from competitors during his early show career. One judge held him up and declared, "This, is an excellent example of a Havana Brown," as some in the audience snickered.

Oh, the indignity, but once he came into himself, well, just call him "Mr. Charles!"

Charlie and I shared a lot of carrot cake during our two years together. He liked the cake and loved the creamy icing. Me? I loved both!

Every time I think about him I have flashbacks to all the good times we shared. Flights to Cat Fanciers' Association shows in the company plane so that I could be back in the office first thing Monday morning, Charlie serving as copilot as he sat in the right-hand seat next to Keith, our pilot. Was this why I was grieving—over my love for a cat and now, years later, two dogs?

That's what Mitch called it during our first conversation after Sabrina died—it was my introduction to the pain of grief and grieving.

What's that, grownups don't cry? Welcome to my world. Love creates unbelievable bedfellows.

I know pets are just pets to some people, but to Mom and me all of you have always been family and we have treated you that way!

Charlie was "my little guy," Sabrina "my little girl," and you Tia, you are my "biggest little girl." Anyone who's ever known the two of you understands.

Mom, Mitch, and I spoke several times in the months that followed your sister's death. Slowly I began to understand why I was feeling the way I did but that didn't mean that suddenly I saw the sun shine, my tears stopped and I heard beautiful music.

Understanding doesn't work that way. Your mind needs time to heal before you can begin to recognize what you had rather than what you have lost.

Tia, although you have a rather extensive vocabulary for a dog, I know you won't understand my thoughts as I write to you.

For those of you reading this journal, this is my way of expressing my feelings when I am in pain. My therapy.

Big girl, we have a fight ahead of us and although I may break into tears at any moment over the state of your health, I want you to know that your mom and I will leave no stone unturned, and will travel to the ends of the earth in search of new ideas that will hold back your cancer and the pain, and prolong your life, no matter the cost!

However, just as with Sabrina, I will not allow you to live a life of pain. Cancer will not be allowed to spread though your beautiful body while I stand by and watch. I did not allow that to happen to Sabrina and I have no intention of allowing it to happen to you.

You will not be allowed to whither away before my eyes. If we are unable to push back time in order to find a miracle we will take the next step, together.

You will always be our little girl and you will be treated as such every day of your life.

I will never stop believing in miracles but should it appear that we are running out of time, you will rest your head in my lap as Dr. Bivens sends you home, where God and your extended family in heaven will be waiting to greet you as you cross the Rainbow Bridge.

When that final shot is given and you are sleeping peacefully I will wrap my arms around you and hold you tight. My body will be shaking and my tears will be washing over your beautiful coat as I kiss you goodnight one last time.

Then, there will be time to grieve.

CHAPTER 2
A LETTER TO TIA

Dear Tia:

Have I told you how much I love you—in the past hour?

Last month you turned four and now I am told you are dying.

I am writing this letter to you, my biggest little girl, knowing full well that you cannot read and won't understand a word of it.

Your doctors tell me that you have inoperable cancer, although to look at you no one would ever know it. They told your mom and me that you have a 10 percent chance of surviving and a prognosis of six to eight months. Well, let me tell you something: when we brought you into our lives you became a member of our family. You are our child and we are not going to let that happen without a fight!

When the doctor asked us if we wanted to have you put to sleep or consult with the oncologist, we said no to both. We needed time to think and to plan, as we had no intention of letting you go.

There was a time shortly after you came into our lives as a nine-week-old bundle of fur that we wanted to send you away. That was because we failed to understand that you were just a puppy, and, even more important, that you were you and not Sabrina, the sister who is now your guardian angel. Once we realized our mistake all of us settled in for what some might call a period of adjustment—getting to know each other."

You didn't make the first part of our journey together easy. You were hell on wheels from the moment you entered your new home and with each day that passed your energy and curiosity seemed to know no boundaries.

Once we remembered you were not a reincarnation of another German shepherd puppy we began to grow together. We never dreamed that in just four years we would suddenly learn that you might be taken away from us and there probably wasn't much we could do about it.

Little by little, before our eyes, you changed from a mischievous child into a full-grown German shepherd lady. I've often told your mother that when you are stretched out to your full length, resting on the rug in the dining room, you look like a porcelain statue. You are gorgeous and the love you dispense each day knows no bounds.

I call you my biggest little girl because you are tall. I called your sister Sabrina my littlest big girl because she was short and long, but to me both of you will always be "my little girls."

When we learned you had inoperable cancer our hearts were temporarily broken—we couldn't believe our ears. That was until we realized there was no date on your AKC papers or a stamp anywhere on your body that read, "Loaned. Return to sender on..."

Given the same circumstances, some people might throw up their hands and give up. Not us. As a member of our family you are entitled to all of the love and protection we can provide. We are in this battle together, big girl, and don't you forget it. We will walk with you until God tells us the time has come for you to return home.

Rather than return to the surgical center to see their oncologist, we have chosen to take you to see Dr. Heidi Ward, the Oncologist/Internist who took care of Sabrina for many years.

We know that, like us, she will not give up on you, and that you, strong-willed child that you are, will fight for every day you are given.

Tia, we will do whatever is necessary to make your life as happy and comfortable as possible. However, I will never allow cancer to savage you. God knows you deserve better. That is why He loaned you to us. Just as with Sabrina, He knew you would be in good hands—and that we would never let you down!

For as long as God allows you to be a part of our family we will see to it that your life is filled with love and supported by the finest medical care available.

As I lay in bed last night looking at your open crate I saw you looking back at me. Your chin was resting comfortably on the pillow just inside the door. You looked so content. Watching you watch me made me very happy. I found myself sneaking a peek every few minutes just to see if you had changed position. You hadn't. At that moment, grief and grieving were the furthest thoughts from my mind.

To me, my beautiful child, your contentment is a sign of the love we share and a bond that will never separate us, even after you are called home.

Rest easy, my beautiful girl. Know that your adoptive parents, as well as your cat buddy Holly, Sabrina, and all our extended family that have crossed over send you strength and love every night as you sleep.

You are always in our thoughts and prayers and we will always be by your side.

Night-night, my little girl—have good doggie dreams.

Your doting father.

CHAPTER 3

SURGERY TO DIE FOR

You think you know yourself?

Believe you can overcome most obstacles. After all, you've done it for the better part of seventy-four years!

Then you come face-to-face with grief and grieving again and your knees buckle!

You probably don't remember, big girl, but it all started on a Friday, shortly after Mom and I returned from a five-day cruise. After watching your lack of interest in food for a couple of days, we took you to see Dr. Bivens. Something was wrong; this wasn't the way our big girl attacked food.

She checked you over and after finding no outward signs of a problem decided to X-ray your abdomen. That was the beginning of my worst nightmare!

She brought the X-rays to the examining room, placed them on a light box, and pointed out that you were in the process of flipping your stomach. This in and of itself wasn't life threatening, but what came next scared the hell out of me.

"Tia is not only flipping her stomach, her stomach is filling with air. If this continues her stomach will reach a point where, if she is not operated on within two hours, she will die."

Talk about a lot to absorb in one big gulp. It was too late to arrange for a surgeon until Monday so she suggested we take you to a local twenty-four-hour emergency center where they could watch over you and, if necessary, operate.

After several experiences with Sabrina and emergency clinics I had little faith in the surgical prowess of these "all things to all people" facilities, much less their ability to pay really close attention to what had just been described as a life-threatening situation.

We declined. I asked her to set up an appointment with the best surgeon capable of performing laparoscopic surgery, which would be minimally invasive. As fate would have it there were only two. One was sixty miles south of us; the other nearly two hundred miles north.

We'd used the University of Florida Veterinary School of Medicine in Gainesville with Sabrina, but the earliest they could see you there was two weeks. Time was critical, so we chose the closer surgical center. We would take you home and watch over you until Monday. We might not be doctors, but we knew you would be in caring hands!

Dr. Bivens explained the risk, but Mom and I knew that no one would look after you the way we would. After being told what to do to keep you comfortable and medicated we left and agreed to see her again late Saturday morning to make sure there had been no change in your condition.

All was well—or as good as could be expected—on Saturday, so we took you home and continued to count down the hours to your appointment on Monday with Dr. Goodrich. Those were three long days, young lady. Talk about grief! Mom and I were walking on eggshells. I prayed, laid on the floor with you, and we talked—as Mom and I worried our way to Monday.

Suddenly I found myself reliving our time together. There were smiles, occasional missteps, and as with any friendship, occasional harsh words. Friendships are like that, you learn to take the good with the bad and over time you build trust.

We go through life making many acquaintances, but few true friends; they are hard to come by.

Our time together may have had some rough spots, but little by little we discovered each other and suddenly you were no longer the little ball of fur that came into my life, you were a full grown German shepherd; and me, I was no longer the giant looking down at you, I was your worried father.

If we had known then what we would soon learn, those three days would have been a cakewalk. I may have thought I'd met grief before, but on Monday we would begin a trip that would bring a renewal of mind-bending mental pain!

Just the other day Mom had said, "Do you realize how healthy Tia has been?"

That's right, big girl, you have been strong and happy-go-lucky since the day you came into our lives. Unlike your guardian angel sister, about the only time you see the vet is for your annual shots. However, Mom's comment was about to catch up with us!

We met with Dr. Goodrich Monday morning. She seemed like a bright young surgeon. She reviewed your X-rays and described what we expected would be relatively simple surgery. But, as with any surgery, there were caveats. In this instance she asked permission to open you up if she saw anything suspicious with the laparoscope. Naturally, we agreed, never thinking there would be a problem.

You would spend the night at the surgical center and Tuesday she would operate.

I don't think I will ever forget Dr. Goodrich's telephone call after surgery and the decisions we would have to make over the next several days.

Dr. Goodrich had found four areas that concerned her and, with our permission, had opened you up in order to take four samples that would be sent out for review.

What was to have been a simple procedure turned out to be far more extensive surgery than Mom and I expected, so we were surprised when she told us that you would still be ready to go home Wednesday afternoon.

We shouldn't have been surprised by your enthusiasm as an assistant brought you out to the waiting room. The minute you saw us you were charged up and ready to go, acting as if nothing had happened and showing no concern for the extensive suturing across your abdomen.

Trying our best to slow you down, we managed not so gently to guide you to the parking lot. That took more muscle than we expected, all things considered. Once you saw "your" car, knowing you were going for a ride was like magic. We couldn't open the door fast enough as we tried valiantly, and as carefully as possible to ease you onto "your" back seat.

As soon as the car started moving you stretched out and went to sleep.

Pain! What pain!

During the drive home Mom and I discussed all of the "what-ifs." If the results of the biopsies were bad we were not going to sit at home with you and brood. We agreed that we would take you to see Dr. Heidi Ward. Oncology and internal medicine were her specialties. If anyone could help us, we were confident she could!

She had taken care of Sabrina, on and off for nearly ten years. During that time she had become more than a vet to us—she was a trusted friend.

When the results came back, Dr. Goodrich called and explained that you had lymphoma, cancer of a lymph node off the small intestine. It was inoperable and could only be seen by repeatedly opening you up.

We had no intention of putting you through that periodically.

Just as we were beginning to take your good health for granted—bam!—our world was turned upside down.

Upon hearing the news we asked the kind of questions Dr. Goodrich had probably been asked dozens of times by shocked parents.

"Could there be a mistake?"

"Are you absolutely sure?"

"Can we send the biopsies out for a second opinion?"

The answers were "yes, yes, and yes," but she was convinced the results would be a carbon copy of the first reading. She was so sure that a second opinion would waste valuable time that she asked if we wanted to meet with their staff oncologist, or would we prefer to put you down, a step she hoped we would not take.

Those were questions we would have to answer by ourselves!

We knew we had to find a solution that would keep us together far longer than the experts were telling us. We were not going to give up on you just because someone said you had little chance of surviving. In our hearts we knew there had to be a better outcome, and as parents it was our job to find it.

Don't let anyone tell you that there is only one definition for the term *grief*. No two people respond the same when they are suddenly knocked down, rolled over, and left breathless. To me, grief is like a hard and sudden slap in the face. You don't know why you've been hit and find yourself wondering if more is on the way.

The anger and pain we felt when Sabrina was diagnosed with cancer came rushing forward. In her case, there was no hope. In yours, we had a chance, albeit a very small one, but 10 percent was better than nothing! There was time for us to consider options that might keep you with us and that's what we intended to pursue.

Damn it, I couldn't believe it. Look at you. Sutures and all, no one would ever guess you had just had significant surgery. No matter how I tried, I couldn't, I *wouldn't* accept the result. I was not going to allow cancer to take you away from me!

We called Dr. Ward. After pleasantries between two old friends, we explained what we knew, and agreed to bring you to her Sarasota office as soon as was practical. In the meantime she asked if we would have Dr. Goodrich release all of your surgical records and the biopsy report.

Maybe there are some things in life that can't be altered, but I am not willing to give in to that theory. After all, how could anyone accurately predict when your life would end?

Besides, they didn't know my big girl!

Although I was hurting inside, I couldn't allow grief to get the best of me and that was no simple task. No matter how dire the situation, or what others might think or say, I knew we had to push forward and stay positive. We had time to try and save you and we intended to do just that!

Tia, we are not alone. It may feel that way, but believe me, at any given moment someone, somewhere, is shedding tears having learned that his special child's life is in jeopardy!

Mom and I had made our decision; you were not going to die—not this time!

My mind was a kaleidoscope, a frenzy of thoughts and actions during those first few days after surgery, but if my voice gave you comfort as we talked then I wanted you to know this: I will *never, ever* allow you to suffer. However, if by some miracle there was a way to allow you to live a good life, one that stretched well beyond the prognosis—one that would allow you to enjoy the time you have left with us—that was what I intended to see happen.

That first drive to Sarasota was difficult for Mom and me. The last time we saw Dr. Ward was in a hopeless attempt to see if she could save Sabrina's life. She couldn't, and here we were once again, looking for a miracle.

When you heard the word *ride* again those beautiful pointed ears of yours came to attention and you headed straight for the door to the garage. Surgery, cancer?

You may have thought you were able to leap onto the backseat, but like it or not, we still needed to be careful as we helped you into the car. We used a sling to assist you and once in, it didn't take long for you to stretch out and go to sleep—piece of cake!

We had no idea what to expect and yet, somehow, we felt that Dr. Ward would find a way to keep you with us for as long as possible. Rest easy, my biggest little girl. We know you will be in good hands!

Between the time we first spoke and our arrival at her office, Dr. Ward had read your files and reviewed the biopsy report. We hoped that upon checking you over she would move forward. That didn't happen.

She wanted a second biopsy opinion. It was a long shot, but sometimes you just have to allow hope to trump your instincts even though in your heart you feel the best course of action is to begin to fight the cancer. After all, time was precious. Still, it was a question we had asked ourselves: could the experts be wrong? We knew we had to rule out a false reading.

It would take a few days to receive a second opinion and, sadly, there was no miracle. Now it was time to move forward. Questions needed to be answered. We were ready to try everything medically available to keep you with us, hoping and knowing that we had no intention of putting you through hell in order to satisfy our desires.

Could we slow the cancer down before it began to overtake your body and we had to send you to a better place?

Once back at Dr. Ward's office we discussed medications, what chemotherapy might do to you, and decided to follow the course of treatment she proposed. Our goals were six months, and eight months, then remission—twelve months. We wanted you with us for as long as God would allow, but knowing what you were up against we would approach this battle one step at a time.

We weren't giving up and we knew that if you could talk you wouldn't want us to.

The idea of you undergoing chemotherapy scared me. I've seen what it did to others, and yet, if that was going to be a part of the solution, I knew you could handle it because you are my biggest, bravest little girl.

The thought of losing you so young was reason enough to begin the grieving process, but when you looked up at me with those deep, dark brown eyes of yours, even my worst fears were set on hold.

Would we be able to eliminate the cancer? If not, could we slow it down—keep it from spreading and extend your time with us?

We may have lacked answers, but we were not going to give up on you, not now, not *ever*!

CHAPTER 4

COULD TODAY BE YOUR LUCKY DAY?

Probably the most gut-wrenching sight I can remember is that of youngsters wearing baseball caps in order to hide their loss of hair. I passed them, one after another, walking in the halls, sitting in their rooms or in waiting areas at the M.D. Anderson Cancer Research Center in Houston, Texas.

That was a picture I never wanted to see again and yet, it is one I could never forget. When I heard the word *chemotherapy* I recalled my time at M.D. Anderson. The only difference as I sat in the waiting room of your oncologist to see you was the fact that her patients had four legs and came in a variety of shapes, sizes, and colors.

I thought to myself, "I hope you are not going to experience a similar result," and then I thought about the movie *Major Payne* and the German shepherd that played a part, and I have to admit a smile came to my face.

I know this was no time for humor, but at that moment I needed something to lighten my thoughts and had no idea how chemotherapy affected dogs. All I knew was having to put you through it was definitely not something I had ever expected to see happen.

As I looked around Dr. Ward's waiting room I saw parents just like Mom and me, sitting quietly, no doubt thinking about their child and hoping for a miracle. We were all in uncharted waters.

Every now and again there was a growl or a lunge. You, Miss Congeniality, took an active part in this exhibition of bad behavior. Even before we sat down you made sure that everyone knew who you were. For the most part, all of us humans were either lost in thought or holding on tightly to leashes.

Could today be our lucky day? After all, this was where one came to find hope.

Cancer! One of the first mental pictures that come to mind when you hear the word is death. Not a pleasant thought. This wasn't a social call. We were here because we'd been told there was a high probability you were going to die.

We were here because we knew that if anyone could help you it was Dr. Ward. We knew she wouldn't give up on you. Every day she fought to create cancer survivors.

Finally, it was our turn to see her. An assistant called your name and after a few minutes we were able to pry you out from under the chairs we were sitting on—and you thought you were hiding!

We followed her into an exam room where she asked Mom and me some questions as once again you took refuge under our chairs, causing me to wonder where you would hide if there were no chairs in the room.

While all of this was going on you did your best to disappear, but it didn't work. Your long nose and even longer tail, coupled with a beautiful long body, made it physically impossible for you to scrunch yourself down in order to avoid being seen.

The idea of our putting you through chemotherapy had its detractors. Some people were already beginning to doubt what we were doing and why. Frankly, I didn't care what anybody thought, didn't know what we could expect from the weekly chemotherapy injections.

When you suddenly had a stomach flair-up after your second injection I held my breath.

The first question that came to mind was, what if you were unable to tolerate the drugs. As it turned out, it wasn't the chemotherapy: You simply had a bout of pancreatitis. Once that was diagnosed we breathed a little easier until we learned that your weekly chemotherapy injections would have to stop until new medications cleared up your stomach problem. More time was slipping away, causing our concerns to heighten— time was both our friend and our enemy!

Would stopping and then starting the chemotherapy again be difficult for you?

Would stopping chemotherapy embolden the cancer and cause it to begin spreading?

All of this was new to us. Like you, we were undergoing an experience that we suddenly found could run our fear factor off the scale!

Dr. Bivens got you past this first obstacle, and in two weeks you were back on your chemo schedule with no apparent side effects.

Once chemo was underway again, I began scouring the Internet for new drugs, forms of treatment and success stories about dogs with a similar diagnosis—anything that would enable us to get on top of your cancer.

It was during this time that I discovered a new blood test that might give us a better idea of what the cancer was doing. I mentioned it to Dr. Ward and showed her the information I had copied off the Internet. She had heard about the TK-1 blood test, but had never used it. We agreed that although the test was new it was worth a try.

The material had to be flown in from the West Coast in a refrigerated pack and used within twenty-four hours. No problem. We were prepared to drop everything the minute we were told it had arrived.

I had high hopes the test would give us information about your cancer, which up until now had been impossible to achieve. As it turned out, it didn't. Well, nothing ventured, nothing gained.

We decided to try the test again at the end of twelve months. How's that for optimism? The first test would be used to establish a baseline for our second and third efforts and maybe provide us with a look at how you were doing.

Mom wasn't sitting still either. She found a homeopathic drug called K9 Immunity Plus, which according to its users was a cancer miracle drug. We mentioned it to Dr. Ward and she indicated she had intended to tell us about it. It was the only over-the-counter product she recommended to her cancer patients. Needless to say, you were on it as soon as we could place an order and receive the first pills.

Have you ever noticed how long it takes to complete one hour—sixty minutes, thirty-six hundred seconds? Now, imagine yourself watching someone you love that has been diagnosed with inoperable cancer and told he or she has a slim chance of living. If you try real hard you can almost hear the seconds ticking in your head.

Sometimes an hour can be an eternity!

Throughout those first weeks, no matter what was thrown at you, you seemed to shake it off and continue to be your usual happy-go-lucky self.

Neighbors were concerned about your progress, but when they saw you, they, like us, could hardly believe their eyes. Sick? Dying? They should have seen you chasing Holly around the house, or prancing around with toys that you wanted us to play with but refused to release!

You were amazing. Nothing had changed. You continued to let us know when every one of your meals and treats were due. There was nothing wrong with your biological clock or your memory. Sick? Not my girl! You were the picture of health.

Well, not quite. The prednisone that should have caused you to gain weight seemed unable to stop your weight loss. During those first weeks you lost fourteen pounds, but never once did you forget when you were owed a dog bone, a cookie, or your favorite—doggie puffs. You may have been told you were one sick little girl, but your memory was working just fine. Should Mom or I fail to be on time you got "in our face" and let us know that there was a schedule that you intended to see maintained.

Having read definitions for *grief* and *grieving* in the dictionary, slowly but surely I was beginning to create a few descriptions of my own, based upon first-hand experience.

Grief is stunning. No, it isn't the *Mona Lisa*. Grief usually arrives along with bad news. It hits you when you least expect it and knocks you down, but often there is time to get back on your feet and remedy the situation. You will probably shed a few tears, but you need to keep reminding yourself that every minute is valuable, so you do everything you can to set aside the mental pain and concentrate upon solving the problem in front of you.

Grieving? Well, that is the aftereffect of losing the battle. Losing a loved one or finding out that a close friend has been involved in tragedy; either way, you quickly learn there is nowhere to hide from its mental and physical pain. You can't will it away; you have to learn how to overcome it!

That weight you feel pressing on your shoulders and the tears you are fighting to hold back rush forward when you least expect them. You feel pain unlike anything you have ever encountered, but in reality it is more mental than physical.

Life comes to a screeching halt as you slam into an imaginary wall, and no one seems to understand what you are going through as you hear a voice crying out, "Why?"

That voice that no one else hears is your own.

There was a time when I thought I was a perfectly rationale adult. Sure, every now and again I would tear up watching sad or feel-good movies, but when I heard you had cancer I cried that first night after you were safely tucked away in your crate sleeping.

One thing I have learned over time—don't be ashamed to "feel." Believe it or not, sometimes a show of emotion can bring clarity to a crisis.

Think of tears as a cleansing agent for the soul. Tears are like a pressure valve; don't fight them. When I released them, Mom was the only one who understood why, and she was the only one that counted as far as I was concerned.

Tia, when you entered my life I didn't stand a chance. Sure we had our problems, but before long you were a huggable bundle of fur and I was yours—almost.

I laughed my way through your stumbling and bumbling and watched as you picked yourself up time and again and moved forward. Like all of the brothers and sisters that came before you, gradually you acquired stability and a personality all your own.

I have always worried about the littlest things that happen to all of you. Whenever I thought one of you was hurting we ran to the vet.

Strange as it may seem, I feel your pain just as I felt Sabrina's.

Over time I came to realize that all of you had been loaned to me for a purpose—to love, take care of, and enjoy for as long as you are with me—and I ought to know: I've lived with upwards of 150 spoiled and pampered show cats during my married life, and now here you were: a second oversize package of love dressed in German shepherd clothing.

One by one our cats departed, but as they left I discovered ways to keep several of them with me. And your older sister, Sabrina, travels with me wherever I go. I pet her when I am troubled and when I am thinking or worrying about you. Some of her ashes are secured in a tiny silver dog bone that hangs from a silver chain around my neck. Just like you, she is always close to my heart.

Anyone who would look in my wallet would see that you share space with Mom; my son Scott; his wife Kiki; our two grandsons, John and Aric; and Charlie, Tony, and Sabrina.

You can't eliminate grief and grieving from your life, but if you want to take some of the pain away, surround yourself with reminders of those you love. A picture is worth a thousand smiles!

As I watch you romping around the house, bringing me one toy after another, I think to myself, "You can't be sick, not my little girl," and I have already begun to plan your fifth Christmas with us, even though it is several months away.

I am glad dogs are not like most cats. You come when I call and come when I least expect you. You love to be petted and rubbed, and you listen as I tell you how beautiful you are.

Although my experience with dogs is limited, I've concluded that they are the polar opposites of cats.

Your amazing memory causes Mom and me to spell certain words and short sentences in order to keep you from getting all excited about whatever we are about to do. The words *car*, *treat*, *cookie*, *peanut butter*, and an assortment of named veggies are guaranteed to see you dancing and barking for action.

Each of your toys has a name that you remember minutes after we give it to you.

The attention you display when Mom and I speak is only exceeded by your desire to lavish us with love and turn every day into one filled with smiles.

My introduction to pets was the result of Mom becoming a part of my life, and the totally unexpected meeting of a dog we named Lokey. He may have been a total stranger and only with us for a matter of weeks, but when he was gone we were heartbroken.

The last words I expected to hear myself say when Sabrina returned home were, "It's too quiet in the house, we need another dog!"

Mom said the same thing when Randy, one of her favorites and our last cat, was returned home. "No more litter boxes, no more cats."

So, who is Holly?

"She's your little sister and you are her best friend."

She's not a dog?

"I hate to be the bearer of bad news, but she's a cat child."

I don't care, I think I'll keep her!

No one should be surprised by people's desire to bring another pet child into their life upon losing a special friend. However, they need to give themselves time to understand their feelings and celebrate their loss.

Sabrina changed my outlook on life. When she was no longer by my side I felt lost and alone, until Mitch entered my life.

In a way, he was responsible for your becoming a part of my life. I called him one day to ask his advice. I was thinking about getting another dog, another German shepherd. He didn't try to talk me out of my desire to once again experience the love and loyalty that was so much a part of my life with Sabrina for nearly eleven years. Quite the opposite, he said, "Follow your heart, and if you want another German shepherd, listen, it will tell you what to do."

And, here I am!

"And we are lucky to have you!"

CHAPTER 5

WHY?

Big girl, were you to ask me to explain grief and grieving, I have, over the past thirty-one years, faced both and do not feel I need to apologize for their effect upon me. My comments on the subject may not be clinically accurate when compared to those of professionals, but they speak to how both have affected me. They hit me hard, didn't go away overnight, and once I came to understand what was happening to me, the answer to the question I asked myself over and over again—Why do I suddenly feel this way again months and even years later?—finally became clear to me.

Looking back, when Charlie Brown was returned home, I had no idea what was happening to me until several years later.

I wasn't with Charlie when it was his time to cross over; I wasn't able to hold him and tell him how much he meant to me. He was in Texas and I was at a meeting in California.

Mom and I had no idea it was his time when I left for the airport. We had known since birth that Charlie was living on borrowed time. He was born with a heart murmur, but our vet told us, "Let him lead a normal life," so we did, sort of.

His passing tore at my heart. Was it my fault? Did I have something to do with his heart shutting down?

We asked to have a postmortem done on Charlie. We wanted to know what caused him to be called so soon. Once it had been completed, the vet told Mom that cardiomyopathy and a heart lining that was tissue paper thin was the cause of his death. In retrospect, maybe I did contribute to his death traveling the way we did to one show after another during his first year.

We will never know for sure, but make no mistake, every day of his life Charlie was one happy little fellow. He never showed any signs that would have caused us to stop his show career in order to extend his life. He enjoyed being shown and he loved people fawning all over him. Who says size is the measure of ones ego?

We allowed Charlie to "be a cat," and he turned out to be a really cool one!

Grief—what was that? Charlie was just "my little guy," the little chestnut Oriental Shorthair kitten that grew up to be a real heartbreaker in more ways than one.

Charlie wasn't much to look at, at first.

He didn't grieve or carry on because he wasn't a success as a show kitten. Each Friday he would walk into his cat carrier and off we would go in search of cat stardom.

People made fun of him as he failed to final in one ring after another, but Charlie, well, he just took life one day—and one piece of carrot cake—at a time.

Maybe Charlie and I ran a little too hard in order to prove that he was special, but then, I knew that from the moment I first laid eyes on him. All I know is that the two years we spent together seemed to fly by, and yet, every minute of it was special to me!

Today, when I read that we should never forget our loved ones, I have only to look around my office to see Charlie, Tony, Wolfe, Sabrina, and yes, you, my big girl, all looking back at me.

Sabrina's cancer came on so suddenly there wasn't time for grief. One day she was just like you, the picture of health for a dog that had undergone an ungodly number of operations during her nearly eleven years. Then, suddenly she was off her feed and within forty-eight hours our vet, her internist/oncologist, and two surgeons all confirmed that her life was ending and it was just a matter of very painful months before she would be gone.

Maybe grief is a good thing. It gives you time to get ready for what comes next—grieving.

Over the years I have promised myself that I would never put a child I loved through misery and pain. Twenty-four hours after her last doctor visit, Sabrina was returned home to meet and watch over our family members in heaven.

Sure, you can find definitions for *grief, grieving,* and *love* in books, but those are just words.

You have to feel their effect to understand their power; you can't appreciate their beauty and pain until you have watched someone that touched your heart go to sleep in your arms for the last time.

Sabrina may be gone, but she is never far away. I speak with her every night before I go to sleep. She is my guardian angel, my gatekeeper in heaven, and the sentry that watches over and protects you.

Every night I ask her to rally our cat children in heaven and the grandparents you never met. I want all of them to watch over you and give you the strength to fight the cancer inside of you.

Tia, you have touched my heart in ways I could never have imagined at the beginning of our time together.

I know you can't understand what is happening to you, and maybe God planned it that way as you attack each day with courage and your usual reckless abandon.

When I lost Charlie Brown, Rachael, Randy, Wolfe, and Tony—your guardians—something inside of me went with each of them. Believe it or not, the pain of each loss was followed by smiles that continue to bring joy to my life. So much so that I will never stop talking to people about "my very special children."

I was the last person in the world to want a dog. I had just retired and didn't want anything getting in the way of my doing as little as possible for as long as possible. Then, thanks to the four-legged stranger I mentioned, I had to have a dog!

Don't ask me why, I haven't a clue.

Don't ask me why, but it had to be a German shepherd child. Nothing else would do!

Sabrina and I walked a road of life together that was filled with pain, pain that would last her entire life—but you would never know it to look at her. She was always smiling!

We walked that road side by side, just as you and I are doing. She never gave up—did not know the meaning of the word *defeat* and neither do you!

Life begins like a painter's canvas—blank, waiting for inspiration that will enable him to fill it with color and life!

Maybe I can't define love as well as a poet could, but over time all of you changed my life and suddenly I knew when I had found it! None of you arrived with guarantees or warranties; only love lasts forever, and it is a gift more valuable than riches!

You, my beautiful big girl, just turned four. You have a life to live. You will not leave me in a matter of months as the doctors seem to think. I will never accept that conclusion!

Unlike with Sabrina and Charlie, Mom and I have been given time, several months to work with—not hours. The 10 percent chance of survival the experts spoke about may sound impossible to some, but to us it is a gift. It means there is hope!

Grief? Yeah, we felt grief when we first got the news. And the surgery! When I looked at you the day we brought you home from surgery there was a long incision across your shaved stomach where Dr. Goodrich had to open you up in order to take her biopsies. Just looking at that incision sent shivers through me!

Your little sister, Holly, was anxious to greet you when you came home, and you did your best not to show outward signs of pain.

Grieving is not something we can run and hide from—quite the opposite. The pain and the tears are like a revolving door, constantly spinning, then stopping just long enough to knock one down again.

This said, having experienced grieving and armed with a better understanding of grief, the example you,

Tia, set each day will push me to be strong and believe in the possible.

Grief! Grieving! Pain! One begins long before the others set you back on your heels.

Life isn't always fair, and sometimes it sucks!

No one really knows how much time we have been granted when we come into the world—except God!

CHAPTER 6

BUT I'M ONLY FOUR!

Sometimes I think we love too much. We watch our four-legged children age, have difficulty with their daily lives, and all the while we tell ourselves, "It's all right, I'm here to take care of you" when we should be telling that loving and loyal friend, "I think it is time for you to make the trip across the Rainbow Bridge to a wonderful place where you will feel like your old self once again."

But I'm only four!

From the moment we learned that you had inoperable cancer I knew that no matter what Mom and I and the doctors did, the length of your life was out of our hands; that's why now, more than ever, we need to stay focused on an objective that may sound difficult if not impossible to achieve—destroying the cancer inside of you!

When Sabrina's time on earth came to an end, her time as a puppy, her school days and how we discovered a way to unlock all of the intelligence that seemed hidden between those two beautiful ears of hers played forward.

The two of you are so much alike and yet so very different.

The letter I wrote to her after she was taken from me provided an opportunity to pour my heart out, to try and understand why I felt as if a dark cloud had engulfed me. I was in pain and had no idea why. Years later, reading that letter reminded me of all that I had gained during our time together and set me on a path of learning.

I'm not suggesting that people sit down and write a letter to themselves when they lose their four-legged friends, but I can tell you that counting your blessings is much better therapy then crying every time you think about what has been taken from you.

Although you, Tia are only four, your years are piling up faster than mine. Dogs and cats age faster than we humans. That's why it is so important for me to remember all of the little things we do together that make each day special.

To anyone who has ever lost a special friend or is concerned about losing one, there is an ample supply of reading material available dealing with grief and grieving. I know, I've read more than my share, but until you come face to face with the loss of a special friend words are just that—*words*.

Without love there can be no grieving.

Tia, we got off on the wrong foot when you came into my life. I almost lost you by comparing you to Sabrina. That would never work. You are your own dog, and I was the one who needed to understand your unique differences as we learned to live with each other.

That's why when you lose a loved one you should never rush into another relationship without giving yourself time to understand and appreciate your loss. It was seven months before we brought you into our lives. We thought that our feelings were understood and under control, but as we came to find out, true love runs deep.

Suddenly, you realize that no matter how hard you try you can't give 100 percent of yourself to a new love, no matter how much you want to.

Mitch was right when he told us, "Your heart will tell you when it is time." It did, several months after we brought you home.

Would it have been any different had we waited longer? Who's to say?

I don't think you ever replace one love with another. No, suddenly you find yourself falling in love all over again and begin creating new memories to add to those you already have.

I want you to know that I am sorry for what happened during our first months together. Mom and I thought enough time had passed, but we were wrong.

There were moments when I thought we had made a terrible mistake bringing you into our lives. It looked as though our decision was not going to end well. We wanted you so badly and yet we didn't seem to understand you, nor you us.

One afternoon while sitting at the kitchen table I looked at my arms and counted the hundreds of spots where your teeth had broken the surface of my skin. Then, I watched you come prancing into the kitchen with one of your squeaky toys in tow, wanting to play, and I forgot all about those spots.

Raising a child, living together and learning to communicate, takes time and effort. Bonding takes even longer, as we both found out. But, when you climb that mountain and look down at the happy child walking beside you, suddenly you realize that every minute you spent getting to know each other was time well spent.

It took work on both our parts before we discovered each other, and then, suddenly, you had me wrapped around your paws.

Maybe it began with the way that you look at me when we are in the same room—you, stretched out and content, your chin on the floor just watching me.

From time to time I find myself stopping what I'm doing in order to sneak a peak to see if you are still watching me.

There was a time when those eyes of yours scared the daylights out of anyone that walked into our house. I'll never forget the time we called Donna, the lady who stayed with Sabrina while we were away, to come to meet you. She stepped into the living room, took one look at you, and said "no." Your eyes had a dark side that would take time to soften—they were eyes that caused people to back up the first time they met you.

Now, those same eyes speak of love and happiness!

Your chemotherapy dates, once weekly, are beginning to be stretched out.

The pink ribbon that holds your bandage in place after each chemo injection is seen less often by neighbors and that is just fine with me.

At night while getting ready for bed I know that if I look over my shoulder I will see you stretched out in your crate watching me. It is as if you are telling me,

Don't worry Dad, I'm on duty even when I am sleeping. Here next to you, ready to protect you.

That devotion has been displayed so many times in so many ways.

Twice while you and I were walking I got tangled up in your leash, tripped, and fell. Both times I landed hard on the asphalt roadway. You didn't run off to explore the area, you stayed by my side. Each time you lay down with your head on my chest and showered me with kisses and once again those eyes of yours were telling me, *Don't worry Dad, I'll kiss the pain away. I won't leave you.*

And you didn't!

Remember the time we came home from a walk in the rain? I placed you in "sit," kneeling on the floor in front of you to dry your paws and coat. Talk about freak accidents. There I was, down on both knees when you decided to give me kisses. Suddenly, your paws were on my chest and all seventy-five pounds of you was bending my already bent legs back, beyond their limits. I cried out in pain and I rolled over onto the floor.

Nurse Ratchet (that's your nickname) quickly assessed the situation and was all over me with kisses and cries of apology.

Was I mad at you? How could I be? You were only demonstrating your love.

That's what I mean about adding new memories to those you already cherish.

Tia, you have always been my protector and I will always be yours. We will walk together as long as it takes for us to shout, for all to hear; "Tia is a cancer survivor!"

The bond and love we share is the same one that made losing Sabrina so difficult. Bonding is special. For some it may never happen, but we have been blessed!

When I leave on Friday mornings for the neighborhood breakfast I know that when I return I'll find you waiting at the door, tail wagging furiously, waiting for me to sit down so that you can leap into my lap and tell me how much you missed me and shower me with love.

When your time comes and you are in heaven, I know that when I close my eyes I will see you, your chin resting on a cloud, those beautiful brown eyes that seemed to sense potential danger long before I did, looking down at me. And I will smile because I know you are still watching over me.

Even when we are apart I send you mental messages during the day, and before I go to sleep I remind you to "sleep well, have good doggie dreams," and, most important, "to be strong and get stronger!"

Something I have learned during my confrontations with grief and grieving is that the enormity of loss is larger than life! I know I can't see the cancer inside your body, but that will never stop me from searching for answers that might save your life. Every night I pray for more time, knowing that one day even Dr. Ward may run out of options.

This is "déjà vu all over again."

For the past three months I have repeated the same instructions to Sabrina, your guardian angel, to rally your guardians and tell them to lend you their strength and determination, to watch over and protect you so that you can fight the good fight, all the while knowing, deep down, that your life may be out of our hands.

CHAPTER 7

ONE DAY AT A TIME

Every morning I wake to the same thought: will today be the first day of the end of your life?

I know it's a terrible thought, but your cancer could begin to move and we wouldn't know it.

When I look at you I wonder if you have any idea what is happening to you.

This thought aside, it's good to see that the chemotherapy hasn't dulled your interest in food or treats!

Nothing has changed. Everything has changed!

You have just come bounding in for the third time, leaping and spinning as you anxiously await Mom's arrival and the passing of the puffs. Now, you are sitting in front of me, ears up, body ramrod straight, waiting not so patiently for me to hand the puffs over one at a time along with the commands *gentle* and *nice*. No teeth are allowed to touch my fingers as you take them.

If I don't move fast enough you will begin talking, telling me in that very baritone voice of yours, *Get with the program—move it!*

We go through this ritual every night. One by one I hand you a puff. If I wasn't watching I might not know when they left my fingers. Good girl!

Meanwhile, Mom is in the kitchen making popcorn for you and herself, and this creates quite a dilemma. You don't know whether to wait patiently until I've given you all of the puffs or run to the kitchen to let Mom know that you know what she is doing and to make sure she has a bowl of popcorn for you once she is done.

You are so spoiled, and it is so much fun spoiling you!

With your last puff received you are off to the kitchen to guard your treasure. Mom is pouring. If only she would just hand you her bowl! But no, you are forced to follow her to the dining room and wait, knowing that in a minute she will begin to spread your share on the area rug.

Here you are, sick as a dog and you can't get any respect. We still make you wait your turn.

Child abuse...child abuse!

Once the popcorn hits the rug and Mom says "free," that long nose of yours is flat to the floor moving like a Hoover vacuum cleaner as, one by one, the kernels of popcorn disappear.

When you are finished, usually in a matter of seconds, you move to where Mom is and, employing your very best posture, and after placing a paw on her lap, you wait, hoping she will share hers. After all, you are sick, but deep down you know that when you finish yours that's it, no barking or crying. All the paws in the world won't help. You have wolfed yours down and now you will have to settle for watching television with us, or simply lying down, flopping over and going to sleep on the rug or in your bed.

Every day begins the same way, with me watching and wondering if we will see signs that the cancer is active. Deep down I know that with each day that passes we are closing in on month six.

Five months have passed and your chemo sessions have been extended once again.

Time seems to be moving faster than usual, if that's possible, and yet I can't stop asking myself, Were the doctors right?

I'm not getting any younger, and neither is Mom. I don't think we will have the strength to bring another child into our life if you leave us. Several people thought we were crazy when we brought you home. So, you can imagine what would be going through some minds if you were taken and we began talking about another German shepherd child.

I should be happy that even with that minor setback at the beginning of your treatment you have charged forward, showing no adverse effect from your meds, but this is no time to rejoice.

So many parents are sitting, waiting in Dr. Ward's office today. Each dreaming and hoping that today they will hear the word *remission*. For us it still seems an unreachable goal, but when we get there—and deep down I know in my heart we will—it will be another twelve months beyond remission before we can rest easy.

You no longer sleep with your crate door closed. After all, you are my big girl and you know that wandering around the house at night is forbidden. Even so, I was amazed how quickly you learned not to come out of your crate, emergencies aside, until you are released by Mom or me in the morning.

Then, and only then, can your tongue go to work, as you look for one of us to kiss. "Wonderful—do it again, and again!"

For me, the first sign of a good day begins when Mom calls you and you are up and trotting off in an instant for your early morning walk. I wait for your return knowing that you will come bursting into the bedroom, beginning to lick my face if I am still sleeping.

Sometimes I hide. You should see your face when you rush to the bedroom only to find that I am not there! But that long nose of yours is all-knowing, and once I am found your front paws are on my chest and I am the recipient of kisses—lots of kisses. It is then and only then that I begin to believe that today will be another good day!

Every night I remind myself to remind you that you must think positively and grow stronger with each day that passes. After all, your extended family, your guardians and the grandparents you have never met, are providing you with love and support as they infuse you with their strength and determination.

Slowly I am beginning to believe that maybe, just maybe, we can win this battle, but then I remind myself what lies ahead.

You take your meds and seem to understand that when Dr. Ward gives you your chemo injection and blood test she is doing it for your own good.

Cancer is a deadly adversary—it kills on its own terms and time. Don't waste any of it; make the most of your time with your little sister Holly. She loves you so much.

And before I forget, make sure you set aside time to rest and recharge during the day.

Dying is inevitable. We humans are so civilized. We create living wills and personal directives that spell out our wishes. You, on the other hand, cannot tell me what you want. Yet, if you were able to do so, I think you would tell me, *Don't give up on me, but should the cancer begin to spread I have placed my life in your hands. I will rely on you to know when it is time to send me across the Rainbow Bridge.*

I am trying my best not to let time get me down, my beautiful girl. My mind is focused on reaching and completing your sixth, seventh, and eighth months. I know that death can happen in the blink of an eye, but we will not dwell on that. Your periodic blood tests continue to show your body is fighting the good fight and the chemotherapy is doing its job.

Continue to push back, big girl. Don't let cancer control your life. Cast it away—erase it from your mind. Strength wins and you are my big, strong little girl. With so much heavenly help supporting Dr. Ward and, of course, Mom and me standing by your side, we are a "band of brothers, sisters, and parents" with a common goal.

Do you remember the doctor's prognosis? "Tia has a chance of living six to eight months"? Well, we are going to stand that prognosis on it on its head. This is no time to slow down or to mope. This is the most important challenge of your life. Be strong. Never forget, and never stop believing!

No one knows you better than I do. Sure, they look at you and know that you are a German shepherd, strong and obedient most of the time. But I know your inner strength.

My writings are based upon what I learned from living with each and every one of you. One day I want to share these life lessons with others. They need to understand that they can get over and then push grief and grieving into the deep recesses of their minds.

However, they need to be prepared to fight with all of their heart and, when the time comes, know what must be done and that they will have a special friend forever.

Doing the right thing, no matter how much it hurts, is what friends do for each other. When it is time for a four-legged child to be returned home its life need not end with death.

During nearly eleven years with Sabrina, I spent untold hours waiting for news from her surgeon that she was going to be okay. During this time I concluded that you children are among God's most perfect creations.

Time and again I watched Sabrina set pain aside in order to demonstrate her love.

I know there are downsides to having a dog. Going out in the rain, snow, or cold isn't fun. Fortunately for you, we don't live in Tennessee any more. Knowing how much you dislike rain and the occasional cold snap even now, in Florida, you probably would have refused to go out until spring, much less step outside to do your business were we still up north.

No doubt about it my love, you are a Florida girl!

Dogs aren't for everyone, though I have come to the conclusion that they should be. If someone wants to reduce his chores he should get a cat, but if he wants to maximize love and affection, someone like you, big girl, is the answer. Unlike cats, you are always happy. Maybe that's why you are called "man's best friend."

Who else would sit in rapt attention listening to my musings or current state of depression, never understanding a word that I speak?

What is a friend?

A friend is someone willing to stand by you when you are down and lend you a shoulder to lean on when you need one—someone who will stand with you through thick and thin!

That's you!

The word *friend* ends with the letters *e-n-d*. Remarkable? I don't think so. A friend walks with you until you are separated by death.

Friends, like love, are forever!

A friend once said to me, "Wouldn't it be wonderful if humans were like dogs?" (Think about it—no, not you Tia, those of you who are reading this.) There is something to be said for the question. No matter how I am feeling you are always ready with a lick, a toy, a paw, or an ear to cheer me up—and you are the one said to be dying of cancer!

Sometimes I think that you have access to an endless supply of happy pills.

Looking back on our early days I find it hard to believe that I threatened to send you back to your breeder or drop you off at the local animal rescue facility. Thanks to your breeder—who informed me that *I* was the problem, not you—I stepped back, took a deep breath, and fell head over heels in love with you.

Tia, you have rekindled emotions I thought no longer existed after Sabrina departed. I think that's why God created you and why He brought us together.

Just the thought of losing you causes me pain. Listen up, big girl, we have a lot of living to do before it is time for you to return home, so let's enjoy every minute of it!

I am surprised whenever I meet pet owners who have lost that special friend and feel no pain, no sorrow. They seem to accept the fact that death is inevitable. When it happens they say good-bye and move on. Today becomes a carbon copy of the days that will follow. These individuals see life as having a beginning, a middle, and an end all neatly packaged and waiting for them. Why get upset about something you can't control? To them, life is a well-orchestrated trip. When it is over, well, that's just the way life was meant to be.

Not to me. Never!

Love is too important for me to take for granted. It is a gift that should be savored, never squandered.

When family and friends are reaching the end of life some of us begin to feel the pain of loss before it is time to say good-bye. Time and again we quietly find ourselves reminiscing, recalling all the good times we shared.

Some people find it difficult to share these moments, fearing they will be looked upon as an admission of weakness—rather than love. Don't pay any attention to them. Tell your friends how important they are to you, how your life is better for knowing them. And, in the case of canine or feline friends, don't be ashamed to get down on the floor, wrap your arms around them, and hug them tightly. Let them know that they are just as important to you as you are to them.

When my four-legged friends depart I've often found myself asking God, "Why are you taking them away so soon?"

That's love!

There is no such thing as an easy loss. That pain that tears at my heart from time to time represents a love lost, but memories cherished.

I feel sorry for anyone who has not experienced the pain of love or taken the time to meet, explore, and express his feelings. Sooner or later the pressure that has built up will erupt in pain that has been held in far too long.

What is grief?

Why do some of us fail to grieve?

Is *grieving* just another word for *feelings*?

According to authors David and Elizabeth Kesslor, grief has five stages: denial, anger, bargaining, depression, and acceptance. That sounds about right, although I've never thought about grief or grieving that way. To me, grief has never been analytical—it hurts deeply and the pain does not disappear overnight. Each time I have lost one of you a piece of me went with you.

I believe you feel *grief*, but you never forget *grieving*.

Thanks to Mitch, your mom and I have come to understand why we felt so alone and emotionally torn when Charlie, Wolfe, Tony, Randy, Rachel, and Sabrina—so many children—were called home.

I want others to understand and appreciate what you and I share, from your first kisses in the morning to the last lick at night before you walk into your crate, curl up, and go "night-night." It's the little things in life that matter most. These are the ones I never want to forget.

I've heard it said that "a trip begins with the first step." For the second time we took such a trip, and eleven years older now, Mom and I headed out to find you.

When we met, you were six weeks old. You were one in a litter of seven German shepherd puppies for sale—one of four females.

You don't know him, but Forrest Gump is one of my favorite philosophers. He was very astute when he described life. He said, "Life is like a box of chocolates—you never know what you are going to get," and where puppies and kittens are concerned you may not believe it at the outset, but take it from me, he was right!

Hear me, Tia: you will not leave me!

I know I said "never again" when Sabrina was called home—vowed I would never again face the torture of loss I experienced when she was taken from me, but *never* is such a meaningless word.

The first time we met you didn't try to hide. You were too busy playing with your littermates. You had an orange ribbon around your neck for identification purposes. We had traveled 150 miles to meet you, but at that moment, as I sat on the lawn watching all of you play, I would have traveled to the ends of the earth to bring you home with me.

You were small by comparison to Sabrina, half her size. Your ride home was dull when I think back to our first venture into puppy parenthood, yet you let us know from the outset that you were not too keen about riding in the car. So much howling and carrying on from one so small! Now you act as if you own my car.

I wonder where that came from!

Early on, you were a ball of energy and I was your favorite chew toy. To tell you the truth, the love I felt for Sabrina was missing during our first few months together.

Mom wasn't a big fan of yours either. In fact at one point she said, "I don't love her. I don't even *like* her."

Little by little you began to establish yourself as a clown, a love, and a fiercely protective child. Well, two out of three wasn't bad. After all, we couldn't have you eating our friends when they came to visit.

Months seemed to fly by and before long you learned where and when to display your protective side. You also accomplished something your sister Sabrina was never able to do: you bonded with a kitten named Holly, the little Ocicat sister that looks up to you. The bonding process didn't happen overnight but, slowly and surely, "Bonnie and Claudia," as I often call the two of you, became inseparable friends.

I can't imagine how Holly would respond if you died. I don't know if animals grieve, but I believe she would lose more than a companion if you weren't here. From the moment Mom takes you out for a walk Holly is at the front door, stretched as tall as her little body will allow, until she finds a clear glass area from which to watch for your return.

Bonnie and Claudia. Frick and Frack. Peanut butter and Jelly. You can't have one without the other—just wouldn't be right.

If we hadn't taken that trip to separate Holly and you in order to see how you would respond when brought back together we might not have found the cancer until it was too late.

Thank you, Holly!

Thank you, God!

Over time I've concluded that God has a place for each and every one of His creations, and once again He chose us to take care of you.

Had it not been for that trip I probably would not be writing this journal. You might be gone, my beautiful girl.

If this was another one of God's tests I'm afraid I don't see the humor in it, but we are not going to lie down and wait for you to return home.

Tia, we are not going to lose this battle. No way, no how! We are in this to win, right, big girl? There can be no second place!

We may be racing against expert conclusions, the odds, and the clock, but we don't have time to feel sorry for ourselves or allow grief to control our lives.

Some people think grief and grieving begin at the end of life and loss. They are wrong.

Both are lurking deep within us—capable of taking us down at any time unless we are willing to fight back.

Grieving is hell times four, five, or six. It does not begin on schedule and doesn't leave shortly after arriving. It can hold you down forever if you let it. Having been there before I know what it can do to your mind. How it can change your outlook on life and people—sometimes forever.

No words can adequately describe grief and grieving. However, once we recognize the symptoms we can turn these mind-bending experiences around by remembering the love we shared—and thank God for the time we were given.

CHAPTER 8

THE TWILIGHT ZONE

Tia, close your eyes and trade places with me. Imagine that you see what I see. Look, over there, you are running toward me, tail wagging, looking strong and happy!

Sometimes I feel as though I am living in the Twilight Zone. I think I see you and then I don't.

During the next few months we are going to take a very important trip, through months six, seven, and eight. I should be doing backflips, but I am scared to death!

The other day Dr. Ward commented that you were amazing, considering how far you have come.

Is our luck about to run out?

Is God satisfied that Mom and I are doing the best we can to take good care of you?

As far as you are concerned, the next few months are probably just days to be taken one at a time. I doubt that you even think about the future.

We have come so far and yet, are the experts right? Will we lose the battle during the next ninety days?

Do I consider each day that passes a gift? You better believe it! Each day moves us one day closer to remission.

Every night I imagine Sabrina going about her task of gathering the guardians to watch over you. I am constantly praising her for a job well done while at the same time reminding her that their work is far from over.

Now, more than ever, she must redouble her efforts! Once she has everyone's attention they need to instill in Holly, your Ocicat sidekick, all of their strength and determination so that she can pass it on to you.

Before Sabrina can complete her nightly task she needs to hold you as tightly as possible so that she can pass her love, strength, and determination directly on to you.

Do I sound as though I am one foot short of a yard?

Maybe, but this is my way of overcoming the voices of doom that I fight every day as I remind you over and over again to feel strong, to get stronger, and to never, ever give up!

Doom, gloom, and doctors—take your best shots, because Tia and I are calling your bluff. We are playing the cards we've been dealt and we are all in!

Suddenly I am worried. Your routine seems to be out of whack these past few mornings. Is there a problem or am I imagining it?

A quick fax to Dr. Ward elicits an immediate response and I can breathe easy—we can continue to move forward. Living with the realization that death can happen in a heartbeat, I find myself overthinking, looking for danger signs that aren't really there.

There are times when I want to grab your leash, hook you up, and head for the doctor.

Believe it or not, I am trying to restrain myself, brush aside the false signs and count to ten before overreacting.

There is no silver bullet that will enable me to settle into the routine we are living together. I am on a roller coaster ride that sees my life going from fearing the worst to feeling that the miracle of life is within our grasp.

My psychology classes in college did not prepare me to face death. They didn't talk about the end of life, or if they did, the discussion probably dealt with family and friends, not dogs and cats.

I lived without concern for so long. Oh, how times have changed!

We live our lives and manage our problems one catastrophe at a time, all the while wishing we didn't have to cope. That's life!

What's the best way to describe moving from grief to grieving?

It is the difference between walking down the street with the sun shining one minute and, the next fog beginning to close in around you. Little by little you begin to feel as though you are in a daze—lost, disoriented, and alone.

Grieving is mind-altering. I'm not talking about the "Boo-hoo, do I feel sad" feeling that hits me in the movies or watching television. Grieving is the equivalent of a mental thunderstorm.

I lost both my parents to a combination of illness and old age within a period of seven months. I felt bad, but I had spent many hours talking with them, waiting and watching as they slowly slipped away. Deep down I knew it was only a matter of time before they were gone and I would never see them again.

When God finally saw fit to bring them home I didn't grieve. I knew they had lived long and fulfilling lives.

I had been concerned as they fought the onset of age and varying illnesses. I knew I would miss them, but I think I felt relief knowing that the pain they were experiencing was gone forever. Their deaths were not times for mourning.

Death, for them, was a merciful end.

Mom and I celebrate their lives, recall the good times we had together with them. Their deaths were not occasions for grief or grieving.

Whether we know it or not, I believe concern is one of the first stages of grief. My parents were an excellent example. I was concerned about them during their later years. At times I wished that God would end their unhappiness. My concern did not end until death took them to a better place.

When we learned you had cancer I thought to myself, "How could God do this to our little girl?"

Fear!

Anger!

I was grief-stricken and grieving at the same time.

Well, I have met "concern" several times in my life and guess what, big girl? I have concluded that it is nothing to get concerned about. We face it—fight it and, although we may leave a small piece of ourselves behind when the fight is over, we move on.

We are not going to allow these next three months to get us down! We were told you had little chance. Well, you are still here!

When the time comes I will take you in my lap and hold you as you go to sleep, thankful that Mom and I were chosen to love you.

I sometimes wonder if there were pet loss grief counselors when Charlie was returned home. Back then the Internet was floating around in someone's imagination, and who's to say that such people even existed? I realize we would not have been able to save Charlie, but maybe, just maybe, they would have been able to help me understand my pain.

I've stood next to Mom many times over the years, watching as for one reason or another it was necessary to send one of our feline children home. I wish I could remember all of their names but I can't and yet I loved them no less than those that come immediately to mind.

As Sabrina moved from one knee operation to another, I didn't need to be reminded of my worst fears—but I was. Every time I saw a dog walking on three legs as we sat in the surgical center lobby, I came unhinged. I was in awe of the strength these remarkable children exhibited, and yet I had no idea how I would respond if I was told it was necessary to take one of her legs.

I don't know what is waiting for us during the next few months, but for now I want to enjoy every day we are together, every day that you are strong and happy.

The next ninety days carry a special significance; every twenty-four hours that pass erase one more day the doctors said you would probably be gone.

CHAPTER 9

I'M SHAMELESS

Where is it written that a cat is just a cat and a dog is just a dog?

Not in our house. Our cats, and of late, two dogs, have been our children since the day each entered our lives.

When it comes to discipline I know all about "boundaries and limitations," and so do our children. Well, some of them.

You can't really train cats. They travel anywhere their spring-loaded legs will propel them—on furniture, into my favorite chair and, of course, onto the kitchen table at mealtime, or wherever food is being prepared. Oh well, little by little we learn to live with them and they with us, thanks to a spray bottle!

Sabrina, and now you, my big girl, are a different story.

You know that coming to the table when people are eating or jumping onto the furniture or into bed with Mom and me is not acceptable behavior. Given half a chance, I would break that bed rule in a heartbeat if I thought I could get away with it!

We seldom have to ask you twice. When we say "place" or "kennel" you move even before we get all the words out. Unlike cats, you girls have always understood boundaries and limitations and that is why you have always been our best girls!

Remission takes twelve months and the successful destruction of the cancer inside of you requires two years of chemo and meds. Right now these targets seem insurmountable, but we have to believe. You have to believe!

How will I mend my broken heart if you are called home? Losing Sabrina was unbelievably painful. Losing you so young would be devastating.

The loss of several pet children has taught me that grief and grieving and the pain of loss diminishes with time. Yet just when you think you have your mind under control you flashback to a memory that leaves you in tears. I tell myself not to be sad—remind myself to be grateful that I am able to recall the special moments we shared and still the tears return.

You and I have talked about the future several times and it has had no effect on your outlook on life. You continue to carry on like the adult puppy you have always been. I wish there was some way I could make you understand that you are in for the fight of your life.

You and I are fighting a disease we cannot see—one I never expected to face again, much less so soon. When I lost Sabrina I swore that I would never again allow myself to feel the pain of loss, but God had a different plan for me. He knew I needed you in my life.

I hope that in your eyes I have turned out to be more than you expected. I never want to own you. I want to share life with you. We are not following defined ground rules. You are a free spirit and I hope that you never lose your playfulness and zest for love and life.

Mom and I were told by both our vet and trainer that we were too old to take on a high-energy dog like you. They said they could find an older, more mature dog for us to love and, believe me, there were moments early in our relationship when I thought they were right.

However, you and I are creating new stories every day, memories for my ever growing scrapbook. Being able to live your life with you has once again provided me with a gift that will last until we meet again in another place.

Looking back I realize that each one of you changed my life for the better!

I will never understand how a human being can rid himself of a family member by abandoning him or her in conditions that all but assured freezing to death, starving or being hit by a car or truck. His intent was obvious: one way or another that child would not be returning home!

When each of you entered our lives I am sure that your new home was a strange environment—probably even a bit frightening. There were moments when we caused you to back away, hide, and at times become defensive. After all, you had left the security of your mother and siblings to begin a new life with strangers.

Whether you know it or not, you were created to be loved and to share love with everyone. Today, a gentle voice, a simple ear or belly rub, or a pat on the head is guaranteed to elicit a lick and reaction that shouts, *More!*

I am constantly asking for extra kisses. For a while I was able to feign crying in order to get an extra kiss or two at night, but little by little you saw through my charade and now you make me work for every lick. Mom says that I grovel in order to get an extra lick or two before you go to sleep. I do. I admit it. I'm shameless.

Shared love has become second nature to you.

As a parent I have learned that I can't hide my true feelings. Every time I have lost a special friend, my life was enriched because I had let my guard down and treated that pet as my child, but with parting there are consequences. My stomach was tied in knots, my head pounded like a kettle drum, and sleeping was done in fits and starts until little by little I was able to close my eyes and recount the wonderful times I shared with each of you.

I think God placed several of His greatest creations in our hands so that Mom and I might experience a very special love, one that knows no boundaries, comes in a fur coat, and is all about giving!

CHAPTER 10
LOOKING FORWARD AND BACK

It seems as though every time we reach the top of one hill there is another one in front of us that is even higher. Well, Tia, today is a day Mom and I feared you might never see.

Eight months, more than 240 days, have come and gone. We still have a long way to go. The cancer remains inside of you and the danger of death at any time still exists. But keep up the good work!

Today is a small victory. We still have to complete twelve months of chemo and meds before you reach remission. It's a daunting challenge, but you can do it. We will do it—together! Grief follows us, waiting for us to falter, but don't sell the power of prayer short. In my heart I know we are being heard and that you are being watched over.

I wish you understood what you have accomplished these past eight months. The odds of you getting this far were even slimmer than we were told, based upon the research I have done.

Several times a day I remind myself to remind you to be strong.

Neighbors love you and stop to ask how you are doing. They don't know about the four-legged family that walks beside you—always!

It wasn't until late in life that I came to realize its power and the price that was exacted as a result of grief and grieving.

Fear!

Anger!

Depression!

Loneliness!

When you are counting days, as I have been doing, your view of "time" changes; life takes on a very narrow, almost surreal dimension.

Every time I feel your kisses on my face I know we are working together.

My life journey with feline and, of late, canine friends has been rewarding in ways I never could have imagined. What those of you lacked in health you made up for in strength, love, devotion, and courage.

It seems like only yesterday that Mom said, "Something is missing in our life." We both concluded we needed another "you."

We didn't rush out to search for you. Somehow we knew the idea of acting on impulse was wrong, we just didn't know why.

Mitch made the difference. He listened. Questioned us. He explained we needed time to heal. He was right: the pain of losing Sabrina did not go away overnight.

Little by little, the more we talked about our feelings the easier it became to open the flood gates, and that is exactly what dog and cat lovers need to do when they have lost a special friend.

Talk about your loss!

Don't be ashamed to cry!

Soon we will celebrate Christmas, a very special one. If I was asked what I wanted, the answer is simple: you. Your being here with us will make the day a joyous occasion.

Sabrina loved Christmas. She could study the gifts under the tree and on Christmas morning go right to hers. She would try in vain to open her gifts, but finally give in and drop one after another in our laps or on the floor in front of us, patiently waiting for us to unwrap and give them to her.

You, on the other hand, recognize that something is happening. You check out the gifts and inspect the tree but you wait patiently for us to open your presents for you. Once opened and handed to you, then and only then does Christmas begin as you squeal with joy and charge around the house with your latest toy!

Each year there are one or more new squeaky toys for you. Once given, you strut, dance, and jump up in the air in front of us. You show off your newest toys, but you refuse to let us have them. I guess you need to break them in before we are allowed to play tug-of-war or toss them to you.

No one expected you to be with us—except us. Merry Christmas, my love!

We have been blessed to have two German shepherds, each with a personality all its own. Sabrina was a submissive child from the moment she entered our lives, while you came aboard and made sure we knew who the alpha dog was. Right away we knew we would have to step up our game if we were going to take back control of our lives.

You tested our patience, and believe me when I tell you that we weren't winning the battle for supremacy and leadership. You were one energetic young lady!

Now, as we look forward to your fifth year with us, you haven't changed much. Oh sure, every now and again you allow me to pretend that I am the alpha male. This transfer of power usually takes place when you want something. No matter; I accept the throne if only for a little while, making sure that no major changes have taken place during your momentary abdication of power.

From dislike to love, concern to fear, our relationship has run the gamut where emotions are concerned.

To anyone believing that pets are just pets, I have news: you are wrong!

Every pet parent I have met fawns over his or her children; worries over them, loves and treats them as family. These wonderful canine and feline children come into our lives understanding not a word of our language and lacking good habits.

Cats have their own agenda.

Dogs, on the other hand, are anxious to learn and please—all we need is the patience to work with them and the rewards are amazing!

That's why you will always be my biggest little girl.

You may have grown into a beautiful, seventy-five-pound German shepherd lady, but I will always think of you as that ball of fur with a colored ribbon tied around your neck—a shy little girl that entered our lives at a time when you were most needed.

I feel sorry for those who have not experienced the unconditional love of a pet. They are missing the joy of one of God's finest gifts.

Pets teach us to care, to feel, and to love. They turn us into better people than we were at the outset of our relationship and we turn them into loving and obedient children. When it is time for them to be returned home, they teach us humility that unleashes feelings hidden in the deepest part of our core, feelings we never knew existed.

In the short time we have been together you have showered Mom and me with love that will make saying good-bye that much more difficult when the time comes.

I am your biggest fan. I smile every time I share your antics with others. The smiles you create are the hallmark of our relationship. If I get up and move to another room I can count upon the fact that you will usually be right behind me.

Doctors say you are dying, but anyone watching you would be hard pressed to believe it.

Is it necessary to lose a special friend to experience grief? I don't think so!

When you flipped your stomach and we were told you could die in a matter of hours if your stomach continued to fill with air, I didn't need to be reminded how much I love you.

In the hands of a specialist we expected your surgery to be minimally invasive, a walk in the park. It wasn't.

You don't have to wait until someone has passed to feel grief and grieving!

The word *biopsy* triggered pictures I didn't want to see—results I was not prepared to hear for a second time! I felt as though all the air inside me was being sucked out. I refused to believe that you had inoperable cancer!

If there is one thing I have learned since being introduced to kittens, cats, and two dogs it is that bad things happen when you least expect them.

When the time comes, believe me, you won't look at those bundles of fur as pets. They've never been pets and—you know it—they never will be. They are family and when called upon for help you will set aside everything else and make the necessary decisions, because your child needs you!

CHAPTER 11

FEAR AND ANGER

Life is a series of events—changes, often without rhyme, reason, or warning, and without your Mom, I might never have discovered the beauty of life and the love that comes with holding a newborn pet child in my hands.

Had it not been for a stranger, Sabrina would never have stolen my heart.

Without you, my beautiful big girl, the miracle of life might have seemed an impossible dream.

I've been thinking about life lately. It must be a combination of aging, the loss of Sabrina, and the possibility of losing you. We have so little control over our lives. We do the best we can, but in the end, life is out of our hands.

Take, for instance, dogs and cats. Who knew they would play an important part in my life? I didn't, and look what happened, lots of kittens and cats, and late in life, two dogs.

I wrote a book in my late sixties, *Unconditional Love—On Loan from God*, a story about my life with Sabrina, discovering grief, grieving, the pain of loss, and love! Much to my surprise, people bought it and liked it. It tugged on their heartstrings just as Sabrina had mine. And here I am, at seventy-four, writing a second story—this one about you, my beautiful girl.

No, you aren't gone, but just as cancer took Sabrina late in life, it has returned once again—doing its best to take you away from me far too soon.

My new career, late in life, won't overshadow a moon shot or world peace, but my battle with grief and grieving is a story I just knew I had to tell.

One of you was oversize and the other undersize, but both of you made yourself known instantly. Sabrina barfed in the back of Mom's new car on the ride home, while you—well, for one so small, you howled like an elephant in heat, and I've never heard an elephant in heat howl!

Both of you impressed your new parents.

Life is full of twists and turns. Living with Sabrina, and now you, have been experiences I will remember until such time as I am once again united with all of our pet children that have crossed over the Rainbow Bridge.

More than a few of you have tested our hearts and resolve, but during those times of stress Sabrina and now you have proven to be warriors. No matter the challenges life has thrown at you, Tia, you shook them off and moved forward as if nothing happened.

How do you do it?

Tia, the strength you demonstrate after months of chemotherapy and meds is amazing. Given the same circumstances, I'm not sure I would have the energy you display day in and day out.

Both of you have taught me to believe in a higher power. I never doubted, but until the two of you came into my life I felt but did not feel!

I've watched the two of you grow, and the transformation has been spectacular. Along the way both of you have demonstrated that love has no end.

The other day, out of the blue, Mom showed me pictures of Lokey that I didn't know existed. Memories came rushing back. His head was so huge and he looked so sad. It was as if he knew his owner was never coming back for him, and yet, although he hardly had time to know us, he was a loyal and lovable lug.

As I looked at his pictures I knew that our finding a home for him had to have been part of God's plan for us. Only a miracle brought Lokey to our doorstep because finding our house was no simple task. We lived on a wetlands, surrounded by forest and tobacco fields. Some said we were out in the boonies, but we didn't care—we loved it.

Had it not been for Lokey we would have missed out on living with two of God's finest creations!

There was a moment not long ago when the doctor asked, "Would you like us to put her down?"

Thank God, we didn't.

Now I look at you and can't believe my eyes. If what Mom and I are witnessing is the expert's idea of you dying, I hope your current condition lasts forever!

Making the decision to end a life is something no one should have to decide, but no one ever said, life was easy. We can't run from our responsibility any more than we should rush to take action because death appears to be the only answer.

Tia, time has taught Mom and me that you need to be willing to embrace your fears, turn your pain into love—a symphony of life!

There is a beauty to death when it takes place for all the right reasons. I realized this shortly after Sabrina went to sleep in my arms.

We should never allow ourselves to be pushed into making that "last decision," any more than we should run from it once we know in our hearts it is time.

Coming to terms with loss often requires help. Today churches, local hospice and pet loss support services can help, but one has to be willing to reach out. Believe it or not, sometimes talking to a stranger, or sitting amid a group of dog and cat lovers who have just gone through the same experience makes opening your heart easier. Once you do, you will be glad you did.

When your sister was returned to God, taking that first step—picking up the phone and through nonstop tears attempting to tell a voice on the other end of the line what I was feeling was no walk in the park.

Mitch was one of many very special grief support people who are available and willing to talk with people like us if only we will reach out for help. They understand what we are going through because many of them have traveled the same road, have faced the loss of a special canine or feline friend.

Tia, we will do everything in our power to keep the cancer from spreading, but should the time come we will do what is right. For now, big girl, don't pack your bags because you are not going anywhere!

Some people will never understand what both you and Sabrina have meant to me. That's their loss. I will not allow anyone to diminish the love we've shared because they fail to realize that you are my children!

Mitch was a gift. He didn't recite chapter and verse from psychology textbooks devoted to death and grieving. He spoke with feeling, and lent us a shoulder to lean on, cry on. As I began writing this journal I realized that one day I might need another Mitch. Coming to terms with the loss of a loved one should not be done alone.

I hope I never become so unfeeling as to look upon the death of a loved one as just part of life's process.

I want readers to come away recognizing the symptoms of grief and grieving, and willing to seek out a Mitch of their own.

Grieving is a natural process. Painful, yes, but it can only hold you captive if you are unwilling to understand its power; —step forward and overcome it!

All of us are born with fear and anger mechanisms when it comes to losing those we love. We may react differently, but that doesn't make us strange; it simply proves we are human.

Shortly after we learned you had cancer, I had the opportunity to sit in on a new pet loss support program offered in a group format. It didn't work for me. There was no give and take. The leader lacked humility and feeling. Participants found themselves talking, but no one was leading the conversation or attempting to reach deep into their souls or the souls of others.

As I think about the hours Mom and I spent at that seminar I realized why Mitch was so special—he had been where we were. He wasn't talking the talk, he was speaking from the heart, and that's what made what he had to say so meaningful, so special.

I suddenly found myself recalling all of the little things Sabrina did to brighten my day. Writing is my therapy; it affords me an opportunity to see myself in a different light, explore the feelings I had as we fought to keep her with us.

You can't keep grief and grieving inside of you. If you do, they will eat you alive!

Cancer kills!

Every minute we share is precious.

Six months. Eight months. A 10 percent chance of living. Words can't kill you.

The leader for that counseling seminar had gathered information from textbooks and whatever she could find on the subject of grief and grieving using Internet search engines. She was well-armed with data.

The seminar attendees spoke of pain, anger, and fear. She plowed through her findings, one sentence and clinical paragraph after another. Her effort to help the attendees better understand the grieving process was lost in minutia.

When someone you love dies, the last thing you want are words. You want understanding—a hand to pick you up and enable you to move forward.

The group leader could not comprehend what the seminar attendees were feeling. Try as she might, she failed to establish herself as a caring friend. She was unable to build a bridge that connected to her audience, and the program collapsed. She meant well but when she was done, the pain the attendees were facing was still there.

Several women couldn't understand why their friends and relatives looked at them strangely, treated them with dismay and frustration when they tried to discuss their feelings.

One woman described how her family all but laughed as they ignored her pleas for help and understanding. They pushed her away, failing to realize that her pain was very real and deep-seated, that at any moment she might break into tears. To them, her Molly, Butch, or Sweetie was gone, and that was that; get over it!

Tia, the battle we are fighting is providing me with an opportunity to reach out to canine and feline lovers who are hurting or find themselves facing an end-of-life decision. Although your prognosis weighs heavily on my mind, I know there are people who can help me face the pain of loss when the time comes.

Losing a loved one can bring you to your knees in tears.

Don't let the term *loved one* throw you. That special canine or feline friend—you know, the one who has been loyal and forgiving, who overlooked your shortcomings for so many years—is indeed a loved one.

When you entered my life I hoped you would enjoy a happy and healthy life, and would never come face-to-face with a life-threatening situation.

Difficult times happen.

My greatest fear is that I will wake up one morning to find you have been called home without my being there to hold you in my arms at the end of your time and tell you how much I love you. That would tear at my very being.

The people best equipped to understand what we are going through are those individuals facing a similar challenge. We meet them every time we take you for your chemotherapy and blood work. They are scared, and like us they are doing their best to set pain aside and focus upon the needs of their child.

I find myself sharing the joy of each parent who receives news that his child's cancer is in remission. All of us know we haven't won the battle, but every success gives us hope!

Each night I make a feeble attempt to let you know how much you are loved and that we are doing everything possible to see you through this, the gravest of diseases, as I kiss you on your forehead and remind you that you are never alone.

To you life hasn't changed much, save for the meds you take and repeated trips to the vet. That is a blessing. You attack each meal and upon emptying your bowl trot over to the refrigerator and sit patiently waiting for a carrot and an ice cube treat.

At six or seven in the evening, if Mom or I fail to deliver the appropriate treats, we can expect you to be front and center either talking to us or attempting to climb into our laps so you can get up in our face and remind us to *do our job*.

After all of this hard work you munch and crunch, stretch out, and crash, your long body resting on the area rug in the dining room. Sleep, my love, it will make you stronger.

You are living proof that our pet children move from one day to the next without a care in the world, placing their trust in the hands of we humans to make the next twenty-four hours uneventful.

Every day that you are your old self is an irreplaceable gift that allows me the opportunity to continue my search for a solution to your cancer. I have apologized to Dr. Ward for playing "doctor detective," but I will never stop attempting to learn. After all, we are in this together!

The other day I spoke with the German Shepherd Dog Club of America which is working with pharmaceutical manufacturers to find new drugs to help fight cancer in large dogs. I reviewed the association's research papers and was told to check back from time to time to see if anything new, applicable to your form of cancer, had been released.

I also looked up the neurosurgeon that took care of Sabrina. Dr. Heidi Barnes was the chief resident in neurosurgery at the University of Florida School of Veterinary Medicine seventeen years ago. Although her specialty was not cancer, I hoped she might be able to provide us with ideas from the academic world.

She had moved on to the University of Wisconsin School of Veterinary Medicine in Madison. She not only remembered your guardian angel sister, she recommended we contact the folks at the University of Colorado Veterinary School, indicating that doctors there were breaking new ground in cancer research and she hoped they might be able to help us.

Not a night goes by that I don't pray that tomorrow will be a repeat of the day about to end.

Live each day to the fullest, my beautiful child, and tomorrow we will start all over again, having put another day behind us!

CHAPTER 12
HAPPY BIRTHDAY!

I am so proud of you that I am almost at a loss for words.

You did all the work while Mom and I worried, but would you believe three milestones are behind you?

Christmas was a smashing success. You were one happy, crazy child!

New Year's was spent with all of us watching TV. You and Mom shared popcorn. Well, not really. You inhaled yours then tried your best to talk her out of some of hers.

Then came the biggest date of all, your fifth birthday, followed shortly by the completion of your first twelve months. Wow! Twelve months are behind you and full remission is just twelve months away. Amazing—truly outstanding!

When we began this battle there was a high probability you would never see your fifth birthday.

You've taken all the needles and pills without so much as a whimper. The chemotherapy that we were concerned would cause all sorts of problems didn't. Instead, lots of pink ribbons have come and gone; time marches on! You still try to hide from Dr. Ward, but everyone in her office is on to you. They simply look under the chairs and there you are.

Reaching your fifth birthday may seem insignificant to some, but when my research indicated that big dogs had a limited life expectancy, well, break out the dog biscuits, it's party time!

This past year has been mentally and physically difficult for us, but for you—nothing to it! When we reached month six I wanted to close my eyes and hold my breath for ninety days. Each day coulda, shoulda, mighta been your last. But not you—you bounded through the black months, as I called them, as if they weren't even there, while Mom counted the time remaining before they were behind you.

Dr. Ward continues to marvel at her "miracle girl."

Well, now that I am through gloating for both of us we need to place our feet firmly on the ground and get on with the business at hand—year two!

This adventure is far from over. Your situation could flip, excuse the pun, and see us back at square one, beginning all over with the next form of chemo. So, let's march forward with confidence and just a little concern thrown in to keep us on an even keel.

What a year!

You have no idea how much we love you, big girl. With a lot of help from your friends in heaven we will bound forward. They still have work to do. They need to continue watching over you and giving you their strength and determination so that you can continue to fight the good fight.

I still feel the need to ask questions and to research your cancer for any new discoveries. I continue to feel as though I am standing on the edge of a cliff looking down. You still require chemotherapy every six weeks for the next twelve months, along with K9 Immunity Plus and prednisone if needed.

Dr. Ward reconfirmed the next milestone: "In twelve months I will consider Tia a cancer survivor."

I remind myself over and over again what a miracle it was that we took that cruise.

Those who don't believe might want to rethink their beliefs.

For over five years you have continued to be just a big, fun-loving child wrapped in a grown-up body. Not a day goes by that I don't thank all of the family members that are watching over you.

The fact that you were handed a death sentence has seen me fight my way though so many mood swings:

Love.

Concern.

Tears.

Smiles.

Turmoil.

And yes, mental and physical pain.

Today it is not uncommon to read about cancer survivors; modern medicine has come a long way. But I don't think there is a book that tells you how to react when you learn that your child has inoperable cancer that can only be seen through repeated surgeries.

Your battle began with chemotherapy and prednisone. One can add weight while the other weakens your bones. At times I wondered which was harder on you, the cancer or the medications?

Mom and I never stop watching and worrying over you. Any sign of vomiting, diarrhea, soft stools, weakness, or lack of appetite and we head for the fax machine. Dr. Ward always responds promptly. However, like so many doctors, she obviously went to the Doctors School of Handwriting and more often than not, we have to call her office for a translation. Oh well.

Some people may wonder why we were willing to put our lives on hold for two years and why we will never board you. Your immune system has been compromised by the chemotherapy and we love you too much to risk unnecessary exposure.

There are still no guarantees where your cancer is concerned. We are not out of the woods yet. The current chemo has worked so far, which is why I wanted to see it continued during your second year.

We repeated the TK-1 blood test that was used last year to establish a baseline at the beginning of your treatment.

My latest research uncovered two drugs that might be valuable should the chemo stop working. I sent the information on to Dr. Ward, but for now, let's hope we never have to resort to them.

Since we began our trips to Sarasota, talking with other pet owners has helped to settle our nerves. Our small group keeps changing, but one thing never does: we all have one thing in common—hope for a miracle.

While sitting in the waiting room I have watched one pet child after another leave Dr. Ward's office with cancer in remission. The growth of the cancer has been slowed, but like yours, the battle is far from over.

Each night I turn out the light and we descend into darkness and go to sleep.

I make no apologies for the many times I have invaded your space at night, as head and shoulders I crawl into your crate to tell you how much we love you and to sleep well, have good doggie dreams, and picture yourself cancer free and stronger. Then I rub your ears, kiss you on the forehead, and climb into bed, where I watch you watching me until you have laid your head on your pillow and gone to sleep. You look so peaceful. I love it!

There have been times when I pictured us walking in a long, black tunnel searching desperately to find some light. But lately I am beginning to see a ray of light at the end of the tunnel. Maybe it's because your TK-1 results came back and you were a 7—high, but still in the safe range.

Sleep well my little girl, we still have a long way to go—another mountain to climb!

CHAPTER 13

THE LITTLE BOX

Pills, pills, pills, have we got pills! Round ones, long ones, circles and squares—they come in all sizes and shapes. We've got pills for most everything in life: a stomach ache, headache, constipation, and an ungodly variety of aches and pains. Got a problem? Just ask—no problem!

So, tell me, why isn't there a pill that can cure the pain of loss? Why can't we just run to our doctor for a prescription that reads, "Take two for the blues and carry on"?

Makes sense to me!

You and I have been on a fifteen-month ride, with more ups and downs than a roller coaster. You've handled the chemotherapy, prednisone, and K9 Immunity Plus as if you were suffering from a hangnail rather than inoperable cancer.

By all rights, my beautiful child, you shouldn't even be here. The professionals gave you a 10 percent chance of survival. Yet, here you are, in remission, going on fifteen months. The prednisone was reduced and then discontinued two months ago, and that was just fine with Mom and me. Your regular blood work continues to look good.

You treat every day as if nothing is wrong, while we face the stark reality that no matter how good you look we could be forced to start all over again.

Don't get me wrong. Mom and I are happy beyond belief, but that doesn't alter the fact that for us, every day is a new beginning. We know what cancer can do, we've been there before. That's why we treat each day as if we were walking on eggshells.

When I was handed a metal box that contained Sabrina's ashes it took more than a few deep breaths to keep from crying out. The short drive home with that box on the seat next to me was pure hell, as every few minutes I looked over at the box sitting on the passenger seat and saw her smiling face.

By the time I pulled into the garage my mind was made up: there was no way I was going to leave my little girl in that box. No way, no how. I had a beautiful porcelain cookie jar with the heavily embossed face of a German shepherd on the front of it. I use to hide special treats in there for the times when she joined me while I was working in the office. That will be her resting place for now.

Several years ago we began using cremation as a means of keeping several of our pet children with us long after they were gone. Believe me when I tell you that although it seems like a great idea, it takes some getting use to. One minute the love of your life is seventy-five pounds of strength and beauty wrapped in fur, and the next you are being handed a box containing a few pounds of ashes; all I can tell you is to remember what she was, not what she has become!

Mom and I were unable to take Charlie and Wolfe's remains with us when I retired and we moved from Texas to Tennessee and finally to Florida. We had buried their remains in the backyard of our home in Texas, never thinking that we might one day want to move them. By the time that day came it was too late; only Charlie's marble headstone remained.

We carried that marker with us from house to house until we settled in what we hope will be our final home. In order to remind us of Charlie and Wolfe we established a small memorial garden in our front yard: Charlie's headstone and a two-foot statue of St. Francis of Assisi, the patron saint of animals, mark the spot where the body of Jessica, a very special female Oriental cat, is resting. We like to think that St. Francis watches over all of them and is a constant reminder of the wonderful cat children that have brought joy to our lives.

If you go before me, big girl, you will join Sabrina, Tony, and me when it is my time. We will all take one last ride together before our ashes are deposited in the Gulf of Mexico. Some of your ashes will have already been placed in a silver dog bone just like Sabrina's and added to hers on the silver chain I never take off. The two of you will always be close to my heart and when our time comes, their ashes will go with us as well.

The loss of a loved one is an excellent time for reflection. Sadly, too many of us fail to find the time to step back and take stock of our lives and what has been important to us.

Tia, for as long as you have Mom and me watching over you, be happy, but for Pete's sake quit ruining tennis balls! Mom bought you three the other day, and you ruined all of them within twenty-four hours. When I was young my dad use to remind me when I failed to take care of my possessions that "money doesn't grow on trees"— and in case you haven't noticed, neither do tennis balls!

Your chemo injections continue every six weeks and you take K9 Immunity Plus three times every day.

I was a late-blooming dog lover. It was totally unexpected, but then, sometimes the best surprises are the ones you never expect. Developing a love for dogs was one of the best accidents that ever happened to me.

Mom and I have experienced the loss of several very special pet children, but it wasn't until losing Sabrina that we came to understand and appreciate the unconditional love that we have been so fortunate to experience over the years.

This journal is not intended to be a "how to grieve" or "how will you know when you are grieving" book. We face loss on our own terms and in our own ways. I simply want to share the fight you are waging with cancer and what we learned when cancer took Sabrina's life. Maybe what I have learned about grief and grieving will help others to make difficult life decisions for their special friends, and help them to prepare for what comes next.

As difficult as it is to watch a loved one being returned home, there is a beauty to it as you begin to recall all of the good times you shared. They will last forever if you are willing to open your heart.

Never beat yourself up over the things you might have done differently. Sometimes, all you can do is all you can do.

Don't allow others, failing to understand what you are going through, to hurt you out of ignorance. Hold on to the love you have lost.

Author Sharon O'Brien wrote about five steps that can help you to navigate the loss of a special friend and overcome the grieving process:

Accept that your loss is real.

It is okay to feel pain.

Begin to adjust to a life without the deceased.

Find a place in your heart for your loved one and allow yourself to move on.

Figure out what to do with your life.

Hopefully her thoughts will help others to better understand and appreciate their losses.

For nearly fifteen months I have gone to sleep at night, never knowing what tomorrow would bring.

I continue to ask for help—help to strengthen our resolve and to look after you, Tia. Sabrina and your guardians have never let me down. Losing her, along with Charlie and Tony, is a constant reminder of just how lucky I have been.

Tia, when it is your time to cross over the Rainbow Bridge I won't care if there are five, seven, or one hundred stages of grief and grieving just as long as I know that we made your time with us special!

The dictionary definition of *grieving* doesn't do it justice: "to cause one to have to suffer the heavy burden of loss."

A heavy burden? This pales by comparison to what I felt when Sabrina was taken from me and when we learned that you had cancer. In your case, grief arrived like a bolt of lightning—and a clap of thunder. My pain grew until I realized there was still a slight chance we could beat the cancer. To some that may not sound like much, but it gave me reason to hope!

Something has been happening to me these past few months, something I can't quite put my finger on, but little by little I have begun to feel as though our lives are intertwined. It is as if we are living in each other's body— living for each other!

Time is our friend and time is our enemy.

I wish that I could control time, cause it to stand still, but I can't.

Total remission, winning the battle with cancer, once an impossible dream, suddenly seems attainable. Fifteen months have passed. Don't look back, picture yourself a cancer survivor. If you can see it, we can achieve it!

CHAPTER 14

THAT'S LOVE

When I think about what you have accomplished, medically speaking, and the fact that you are closing in on eighteen months, I am reminded of words written by Elizabeth Barrett Browning: "How do I love thee? Let me count the ways."

I love to watch you watching me.

I love to watch you playing with your sister—watch the two of you snuggling close together if only for a few minutes. Should we look your way, it is as if you don't want Mom and me to know how much you care for each other—you separate immediately.

I love to watch when you go into your protective mode, although at times you can get a little loud. Sometimes I think you go there just to let me know that you can.

I love the way you remember the time for each and every dog treat, meal, and walk. Should we forget, you get up close and sit and stare at us. If we fail to respond you whack us with your size fourteen paws and, as a last resort, you attempt to climb into our laps, get nose to nose, and begin kissing us furiously.

I love the way you remember the names of each and every one of your toys and the fact that we have to spell certain words and phrases in order to keep you from getting excited.

Tia, you make each and every day one of laughter and joy. There are times when words fail me as I try to describe your latest antics. So much love! So many laughs, and yes, more than a few tears, but you are worth each and every one of them.

I am so fortunate to have been given this time with you. Eighteen months. Think about it: you should have been gone a year ago!

Whatever God chooses to do in the future will not change the fact that I have been blessed to have had you with me far longer than anyone could have imagined. When we began this fight I was afraid it might be over quickly. That wasn't the attitude or the support you needed from me.

The other day I communicated with Dr. Ward via fax about some little signs that were bothering me. At times you seem to be sluggish, not your usual high-spirited self, and the pads on your feet are slick, affording you little protection during walks on hot days, to say nothing of a lack of traction when attempting ninety-degree turns. You end up sliding into walls as you chase your little sister Holly through the house. I know I shouldn't laugh as you pick yourself up and continue this fruitless effort, but I can't help myself, it's fun to watch. She really smokes you!

In the fax I suggested that Dr. Ward consider doing an ultrasound in an effort to make sure the cancer is not spreading. It may not tell us much, but we shouldn't allow that to stop us from trying to stay ahead of it.

She agreed, and in her response suggested we repeat the TK-1 blood test. That is just fine with me as you are almost halfway to full remission; it's a good time to take another look.

Sometimes during quiet moments my mind wanders, and lately I find myself thinking how much alike you, Sabrina, Tony, and Charlie are and yet so different. Pain and fear is the common denominator. None of you have allowed it to slow you down!

Many years ago I decided to share two letters that I wrote to myself about Charlie with the Cat Fanciers' Association monthly publication. I wanted everyone in the cat world to know how much I loved him. The feedback I received from breeders and friends was heartwarming.

The letter I wrote to myself about Sabrina resulted in the book *Unconditional Love—On Loan from God*. Just as with Charlie's letters, the reader feedback has resulted in more than a few tears.

Much to my distress, I came to realize that none of you has ever been mine to keep. It has been up to me to make the most of the time we were granted. Mom and I have always done our best, and yet every time it became necessary to let one of you go, it seemed so unfair!

Can you spell *d-e-p-r-e-s-s-e-d*?

With Charlie, Tony, and Sabrina, recalling all that they meant to me has helped to ease the pain of loss.

Sometimes when I am down I close my eyes and recall all of the good times we had together, and I am better able to appreciate what you children had gone through. The surgeries you required, your strength and resiliency leaves me breathless.

Time and again I listened as Sabrina's surgeons described what could happen during surgery, and later, how careful we had to be when she was returned to us, before they headed back to the surgical kennels to bring her out.

No matter the surgery or the number of days she remained at the surgery center for aftercare, they could not contain or restrain her enthusiasm once she saw us.

You responded the same way after your stomach surgery.

And, Charlie?

We will never know if that little guy was in pain; for two years he lived every day to the fullest.

That's love.

That's beyond amazing!

I have no right to feel grief or grieving as long as I keep all of you close to my heart.

God creates amazing children.

Step into the light. Share the joys you feel with others. You can't overcome grief and grieving unless you are willing to release your emotions.

You can never forget those you love, they remain a part of you forever!

CHAPTER 15

NIGHT VISION

We just got a call from Dr. Ward.

It has been a long time since I lost control of my emotions and cried myself to sleep.

I was fine until I looked over at your crate to say good night and you weren't stretched out with your head on the pillow looking back at me.

I couldn't see you. It was as if your crate was empty. Not wanting to wake Mom, I reached for the small penlight I keep on my nightstand for emergencies, turned it on, and there you were, sitting upright in the back of the crate just looking out at me.

As I wiped my tears, I wondered if somehow you knew what we had just learned a few hours ago—but, how could you?

I turned out the light, told you one more time to have good doggie dreams, and fought more tears until my sleeping pill finally kicked in.

Something happened during the night that has only happened once before. I woke from a restless sleep, or maybe it was a dream, I'm not sure.

As I lay in bed looking around, I thought I saw you walking toward the door to the dining room. I called out "kennel!" You stopped and looked back at me. I told you to "kennel" a second time, and when you didn't move I reached for the penlight again. I pointed it toward the door and turned it on. You weren't there!

At first I thought you had gone into the dining room while I took my eyes off of you, but before getting out of bed to bring you back I swung the beam toward your crate.

There you were, head on your pillow, fast asleep.

I'm positive this wasn't a dream. After all, I was wide awake, I think. Besides, this has happened once before.

In the morning I told Mom what happened.

"Sabrina visited Tia last night. I know you think I'm a wack-job, but I know what I saw and no one will ever be able to convince me otherwise. This is the second time she's done that!

"Maybe she felt it necessary to visit again because I was concerned about the results of Tia's TK-1 blood test. After all, I did tell her about the results of the test; I was worried and I asked that Sabrina and the guardians redouble their efforts to protect Tia.

"This all sounds strange, but in my heart I believe she came down to comfort Tia and make sure she knew that everyone was watching over her. Go ahead," I told Mom, "call me crazy, but I know what I saw."

Needless to say, Mom was more than a little bit skeptical. She didn't say much, just listened.

We are in month eighteen, no small miracle and sometimes when something is "too good to be true" it isn't necessarily good *or* true!

What changed?

Everything!

Dr. Ward had called to give us the results of your latest TK-1 blood test, and although she had taken longer than we expected, we were confident the news would be good.

She had had the results for a few days, and explained, "I just didn't know how to tell you."

Then she did!

The rating the first time you took the TK-1 test nearly eighteen months ago was a 3. That was fine. The number we had to worry about was 9.

At twelve months we had repeated the test using 3 as a baseline. The result was a 7. I was concerned, but Dr. Ward explained that she was still satisfied that you were doing fine.

Then came the shocker.

"Tia's test score was 13."

Dr. Ward did her best to allay our fears. She told us not to worry, instead to listen to our eyes.

All of us believe you are the picture of health. You are strong, happy, and a free spirit for sure. Besides, you had been scoped and had a conventional blood test along with the TK-1, and both were fine.

Well, it wasn't fine!

The news hit me hard. I didn't want to believe it. I was not about to accept that something was happening and we couldn't see it, even though I realized the only way to really know what was going on required a surgeon opening you up and checking, and we were not about to do that.

"Deep breaths, take deep breaths," I told myself over and over. Now I understood why Dr. Ward was uncomfortable delivering news of the results.

Then I remembered something Mitch told me: "Believe your heart and don't look back." Those words can be applied to so many life situations.

Tia, as I have told you before, we are not running a sprint, we are running a number of marathons, back to back, so don't dwell on the past, run to the light!

Nothing was ever scripted with Mitch, just an honest and caring voice on the other end of the telephone reminding me how lucky I was to have had Sabrina so long.

"Enjoy recalling each day you were given," he had said. Now that's a life lesson to remember! Recalling his words was a shot in the arm. I was reminded how blessed we have been to still have you with us.

We took you back to Dr. Ward a few days later to repeat the TK-1 blood test and take full body X-rays. I wanted to come away as positive as possible that the cancer was not active in other parts of your body.

As we waited for Dr. Ward in the lobby, one of her assistants brought Mom your X-rays. I think we both freaked out at the same time. Mom asked me, "Do you think we need to take Tia to see a surgeon?"

We couldn't believe what we were thinking.

A few minutes later the assistant brought you back to us. Minutes were beginning to feel like forever. Then Dr. Ward came out. Mom spoke first, expressing her concern, and before she could finish Dr. Ward apologized for any misunderstanding, telling us she just wanted us to have the X-rays for safe keeping and that your body was clear, normal.

Talk about a sigh of relief!

The life lessons just keep piling up: Never take life for granted. Make the most of each and every day you are given because...

Change happens!

Grief is all about emotion—feelings that, like cancer, are often hidden deep inside each of us; strong feelings we never know exist until we are confronted by stress.

Tia, medicine may be keeping you alive, but I believe that love has been the secret weapon that has driven us to challenge what once sounded impossible.

Life is never normal with you around. Please, please don't ever change!

I will know when it is time for you to go, my love. I will *not* keep you by my side for another day, another week, just to please myself. When it is your time, you will head for the Rainbow Bridge knowing that you spent your last minutes on earth right where you belonged, with your head in my lap. And that will help to ease the pain of losing you.

When that time comes, Sabrina and your guardians—all of the family you have never met—will be waiting to greet you, paws and arms outstretched, anxious to welcome you home.

You have never been and never will be alone, my beautiful girl.

I know the pain of loss. I understand the meaning of grief and grieving. There was a time when I asked why, but not anymore; for you see, I have learned a valuable life lesson: grieving is the purest form of love.

CHAPTER 16
TAKE NOTES

There I was, standing under the shower allowing hot water to beat down on my recently repaired shoulder when words started to flow. The words became paragraphs and I thought to myself, "Dummy, you will never remember everything you want readers to know about cats and dogs." Well, mostly dogs, as I mentally apologized to Holly, Tia's sidekick and best bud.

I told Mom about my epiphany in the shower and the fact that I probably forgot half the magnificent prose I wanted to write and she responded, "If I've told once I've told you a million times, take a tape recorder or a notepad and pen with you wherever you go!"

Thanks, I needed that!

My look probably said it all as I concluded that sometimes silence is the best response, but make no mistake, I was thinking, "In the shower?"

Sometimes, silence is a virtue.

I grabbed a pad and pen and attempted to remember as much of my mental explosion as possible.

Why do people bring kittens or puppies into their lives, and what can they hope to gain from the experience? Love!

If your kitten or cat turns out to be like Holly, you will be blessed with a child that wants to be loved, will curl up in your lap for hours, and will look up at you every few minutes through the huge, saucer-size orbs that Ocicats have been blessed with and without so much as a meow, those eyes tell you, *Thanks for loving me.*

On the other hand, you could wind up with a cat that you are lucky to see at mealtime, and then, only for as long as it takes to wolf down its food, then disappear.

Either way, you have selected a child that is easy to maintain. Just keep the litter box clean, change the cat litter regularly, provide a bowl of fresh water when needed; add a treat or two every day, and there you have it—a cat!

I don't have to tell you about a puppy or a dog, you've already met Sabrina and Tia. I can't promise that you will experience the love my two gals have lavished upon me on a daily basis. What I can promise is some exercise whether you need it or not, often in the worst weather you can imagine; and don't be surprised if you find some teeth marks on your favorite furniture or various parts of your body while that itsy bitsy, lovable ball of fur is growing up.

What does this have to do with grief and grieving? Plenty!

Remember the song "How Much Is That Doggie in the Window?" or the TV commercial you saw the other day with one or more lonely dogs and cats staring out at you as an announcer pleaded, "Come save these children; they need a home—they need *you*"?

No they don't!

Not until you've taken the time to answer one question: Why?

What, you were looking for more?

Believe me, if you can't answer why, buy a fishbowl, fill it with water, and tell your friends you've got an invisible fish. No harm, no foul!

I've lived with cats for over thirty years now and, take my word for it, they are like a pair of wash-and-wear slacks. Do what the label tells you and you're done.

I've lived with two dogs for over seventeen years, and don't let that commercial I mentioned fool you. Dogs have needs that require your attention and sacrifice. I called Sabrina, our first German shepherd, a special needs child. Looking back on our time together would I change even one minute of my time with her? Not on your life! During our nearly eleven years together her medical bills ran into the thousands of dollars in order to keep her with us. I've jokingly told friends, "We added a wing in her name onto the surgical center in Largo, Florida!"

Without realizing it, Sabrina taught me about grief and grieving, and by the time I returned her to God I was an expert. I just didn't know it.

Saying good-bye to her was the worst moment of my life. I experienced physical and mental pain unlike anything I thought possible. No, I hadn't been hit by a truck, or gotten tangled up in a leash and fallen down. I had fallen head over heels in love with my little girl.

Sabrina proved that emphatically stating "never again" can last for twenty-four hours and, in our case, an additional seven months—the time it took me to get my head back into some degree of normalcy and for Mom and me to get in some much-needed vacation time.

Then you came into our life. Top breeding, magnificent lineage and, oh, what a mistake!

I thought we had made a mistake after just one month!

We were expecting a submissive, lovable clone of your guardian angel sister, and what we got was Tony the Tiger. A whirling set of teeth! A terror wrapped in fur!

Submissive? Hardly!

It took a while to smooth out your rough edges and acknowledge that you were the alpha dog in the house, unless you saw fit to loan that distinction to one of us for a few minutes or hours.

Slowly but surely you became a lady and turned into a seventy-five-pound love machine. Smart as a whip, and a pain in the butt! You always seem to want me to play with your toys when I am reading or taking a nap.

Then, weeks after you turned four, we learned that you had inoperable cancer. It wasn't fair. Not now, not ever!

That word, *cancer*, broke my heart and brought me to tears. You could be dead in months, maybe weeks, but I didn't know that at first.

Once again there were vet bills, but—as with Sabrina— I would spend my last dime to give you a chance to live a full life with us, one that didn't end too soon! Make no mistake, we're not rich. Mom and I belong to that retired middle class that people talk so much about these days.

No one should bring a dog or cat into his life because he sees it as a noble gesture. He shouldn't expect the "get acquainted" period to last only a few weeks. It takes months, sometimes years before one can learn to live with a canine or feline child.

I believe that you and Sabrina are living proof that God places His special needs children in special hands. If you thought we picked you, and Sabrina before you, well yes, we did, but with a little help from above!

Bringing you into our lives wasn't our good deed for the day. It was for life and everything that came with it. No refunds, no returns—for better or worse—for as long as we were fortunate to be together.

So, television viewers, if you can't take the heat, do yourself a favor—remember the fish bowl?

I know some people will shake their heads and say to themselves, "Who can tell what the future holds, what if at some point we can no longer afford our dog or cat?" Get a fish bowl! You wouldn't throw your son or daughter out in the cold because times are tough, would you?

That four-legged being that looks at you longingly and showers you with affection is a child, too!

I can't be sure these are the exact words that were running around in my head this morning, but it's the thought that counts and now these words have flowed for a second time, just like in the shower.

Tia, there may be times when you amazing children set us back on our heels, the result of a diagnosis we weren't expecting, but that is no reason to walk away from you.

When it happened there were tears—lots of them. And pain—lots of it!

There are times when we needed to stand firm and fight, to do whatever is necessary to get all of you back on your feet. If that requires driving or flying to specialists, or having the courage to say good-bye to you long before we planned in order to avoid putting you through a living hell, well, that's what we, as parents do, no matter how much it hurts.

Yes, I would have given anything for just a few more years with Charlie, Tony, or Sabrina, but it was time for me to keep my promise. It hurt—oh, how it hurt!—and yet, to forget the pain of loss would have lessened the joy of remembering our time together!

Mom and I will be with you for as long as it takes to win this battle, Tia, as long as I know the cancer is not out of control.

I will never take you for a ride in the country, throw you out and drive off.

To anyone smitten by an animal rescue commercial that has you all charged up and ready to rush out and bring a dog or a cat home, before you bite (no pun intended), ask yourself that one question: Why?

The streets are filled with cats and dogs whose owners started out with good intentions. Then, for whatever reason, they found it necessary to cast away these four-legged family members. If you are not prepared to stay the course, get that fish bowl. But if you are looking for a life-changing experience, bring a dog or cat into your life!

Tia, soon you will enter month nineteen and get your next chemo injection, but right now, it is the fourth TK-1 test, which you took nine days ago that we are concerned about.

Well, Dr. Ward called Sunday night. She had the results and wanted us to know that your number had dropped from 13 to 9.5, still in the danger range; but no one would know it to look at you.

That sound you hear?

I am listening to my heart!

Tia, as you know, it helps to have an amazing life partner, Mom, who loves canine and feline children as much as or more than I do, a partner who was willing to step in and take care of all the chores while you, big girl, rehabbed from your surgery!

CHAPTER 17

THE TRIP

I hope I have made it abundantly clear that as far as the harsh reality of grief and grieving are concerned I am simply someone who, late in life, has come face-to-face with both of these mind-altering emotions.

I once told a friend that my first book, *Unconditional Love—On Loan from God*, could very easily have been titled *Life Lessons Learned at the Feet of a Dog*.

Sabrina taught me the meaning of unconditional love. She demonstrated a strength that made my problems look small, and when it was time for her to return home she went to sleep where she belonged, in my arms.

Shortly after that I discovered the true meaning of grief and grieving. The pain of losing her reached every corner of my soul. I felt as though my heart was being torn from my body!

I did not want to accept the fact that this amazing child was no longer mine.

I told myself that I could deal with losing her, but I couldn't!

I can't begin to tell you the number of times I told myself that God had let me down. After all, hadn't I begged Him to return her to me after each surgery? In return I promised to do whatever He asked. And all He ever asked was that I love and care for her, just as I am doing for you.

When she was gone I felt empty. I forgot the love and remembered only the pain!

I know there will be people reading this who will respond, "Get a life!" Wow, so simple, and when I do, all of my pain will mysteriously disappear? Don't let anyone tell you that the healing process doesn't take time. It may be difficult for some to understand the everlasting bond that was created.

At first, I found myself asking one simple question: Why do I feel this way?

Deep down, I knew the answer. Sabrina was loving, loyal, and brave every day of her life, just like you. You have never been just a dog, my biggest girl.

It takes time to come to grips with the fact that your child has only been loaned to you.

Ask me about grief and grieving and don't be surprised if I answer, "Grief is finding out that your child has cancer and only a slim chance of surviving. Grieving is sitting on the floor with your child resting her head in your lap and looking up at you as the first of three injections slowly return her to a pain-free place."

Been there, done that!

You know that she is gone, but you find yourself holding her tightly, unwilling to give her up, as you rock back and forth crying uncontrollably—hoping she knows how difficult it was for you to let her go.

Why?

You repeat that question over and over, and although you know the answer it doesn't make what has just taken place any easier.

We are doing everything in our power to keep from giving Tia up, but deep down we know that her life is not in our hands.

Not long ago nutcases like me had no one to talk with upon losing a special friend. Then, thanks to the creation of pet loss support phone lines, places of worship, and groups that today conduct pet loss grief counseling, people can reach out and find help and understanding.

And you must reach out. You can't fight the pain alone. You can tell yourself you understand what is happening to you, but you don't! You need to find a Mitch of your own.

The pain Mom and I suffered when Sabrina was returned home was beyond anything we had ever experienced, but we were lucky in that we found someone to talk with, someone to share our pain with.

Find a someone for yourself.

Believe me, there are people waiting to help you through the difficult times you are experiencing.

That's right, I said *times*—plural. Don't think that just because you spend a few minutes with someone on the telephone or in a discussion group that your pain will be washed away. It won't!

Even today, as enlightened as we think humanity is, there are still people that look at us as we fight to cope with the loss of a canine or feline friend and consider us strange!

We aren't—*they* are!

Tia, it took Mom and me seven months before we felt confident enough to bring you into our home and lives.

We spent several hours talking with Mitch, shed buckets of tears, and even now, years later, I am still not immune to becoming choked up.

Surprising as it may seem to some people, we chose the same breed. That's not for everybody. You can spend years shortchanging your new child by constantly comparing her to the one that won your heart and then broke it when she departed.

We wrestled with our decision until Mitch came to the rescue. Suddenly we remembered his best suggestion, "Listen to your heart." We did.

Tia, we made the right decision!

Sure, no matter how hard we tried not to, we compared you to Sabrina. It's only natural. We kicked ourselves each time we inadvertently called you Sabrina. But take my word for it, Tia, there is only one of you and we are the fortunate recipients! You have proven to be more than we had any right to expect. You are strong, smart, loyal, and loving.

When we heard that word *cancer* a second time, it was as if a stake had been driven through our hearts! It had taken your sister, but it will not take you, not if we have anything to say about it—which, of course, we don't.

You are twenty months into chemotherapy, and although you are usually a little punky when you return home from your latest injection, the next morning you are up and ready to bound through the day with a smile on your face!

Based on the assessment of professionals and everything I have read during this battle, you could have been gone in a matter of weeks, not months; but here you are, waiting for your nightly carrot, pep talk, and kiss goodnight.

You have just come in from doing your business, raced through the house, and careened head first into your crate, stopping with a resounding thump. Now that beautiful long head of yours is poking out the door looking toward the kitchen to see if I have picked out the largest baby carrot for you.

Lately, you have become quite a tease. No matter how hard I try, you are only giving me a goodnight kiss on alternating days. I moan, I groan, I beg and grovel, but it does me no good. You have taken to hiding my slippers, although when confronted with the evidence you refuse to acknowledge the dastardly deed.

Tia, all you have ever asked of Mom and me is to love you. In return you have showered us with love and devotion.

Don't give up, my beautiful girl; we never will. Grief and grieving cannot trump love unless we let them.

At the end of each day I close my eyes and visit with Sabrina and each of your guardians. I treat each new day as if it is a new year, knowing that tomorrow will come soon enough.

Sleep well, my little girl.

Dr. Ward calls you her "miracle girl," and for good reason. Slowly but surely, one day at a time, our goal is within reach—a pink ribbon, the one that shouts, "I am a cancer survivor!"

CHAPTER 18

NO!

Throughout the battle we have been waging there has been one constant, your demeanor has never changed. You haven't walked around with your tail between your legs, bemoaning the fact that you have cancer. You get up each day with a level of enthusiasm that carries you until you dive head first into your kennel at bedtime, turn around and look to make sure I am close behind with your last treat of the night.

Month after month you have risen to the challenge of fighting your cancer, never believing what the doctors had told us. You continue to love just about everyone except other dogs. This response has been a constant concern of ours, one that has caused Mom and me to start talking about breaking out your old electronic collar, the one we used when you were a youngster in training.

I can't say I am excited about the idea. In the past when I used it and heard you whimper in response I felt as though I was electrocuting you, which of course is not a valid concern. I've never been able to abide the idea of training through pain even though I know the collar is used by many professional trainers.

When you were young the collar worked like a charm, so after months of training with a class of fifteen to twenty mixed breeds and sizes, I suggested that we take it off. It wasn't long before you were back to your old self: a raging, lunging package of fur and muscle whenever you saw another dog. I know your aggression is all bark and no bite, but that doesn't stop me from worrying about your potential for harm.

Well, the collar is back on and a trainer known as "the dog whisperer" is coming out to see you in action in the hope that use of the collar will be short-lived. So far, I have had to nick you a couple of times and in each case you responded correctly. I really want you off this device and am hoping that its use will only be temporary, but make no mistake, my little girl, we are not going to allow you to slip back to your old routine.

As vicious as you appear to be on the surface, and as big a bully as you appear to be, deep down I am scared of what might happen to you should you demonstrate your anger to the wrong dog, because I know you are a fraud. In reality, if your victim responds in kind, you become a frightened young lady and begin to cry. I may know and understand you, but sadly other dogs don't. Deep down, I believe this is your way of showing off your alpha side.

The other day Mom noticed a cyst on your right hind leg. We called to make an appointment to see Dr. Bivens and were surprised to find that she had sold her practice, and although I wanted to take you up to Dr. Ward, Mom decided to try a new vet.

The vet took one look at the cyst and decided to pop it with his fingers as a means of allowing it to drain. He gave us a prescription for an antibiotic and told us to keep you on it for a couple of weeks and said that everything should be just fine.

Well, I, the consummate worrier, looked at the material that was oozing out and to my mind I immediately thought "cancer." I know this sounds a little melodramatic, and when I asked the vet he told us not to worry—which of course went in one ear and out the other. As far as I was concerned anything but the sniffles should be seen by your oncologist.

Two weeks and several pills later the infection didn't look much better, so it was ride time. We said the magic word, *car*, and off we went to Sarasota. To you this was just another ride, but to me, all I could see was gloom and doom.

While Dr. Ward was examining the infection I asked, "Could this be cancer related?" When her answer was positive, your dad was wishing all sorts of misfortune upon the other vet.

Dr. Ward took samples and sent them off to be reviewed. There were new pills and for a few days I walked around mumbling and grumbling to myself.

I know that none of us grow up thinking, "Today I have cancer," but after more than twenty months of living with and watching you fight this demon, even a hangnail would have set me off.

The next few days were spent waiting for biopsy results. Beating your cancer, once only a dream, was within our grasp—and now this!

You can guess how my nightly discussion with Sabrina went. I praised everyone, but told her to hold off on any premature celebration, that we weren't out of the woods yet. Then I went on to explain what had happened and that everyone had to work overtime watching over you until we had reached and passed the twenty-fourth month.

A few days later Dr. Ward called with the results. She told Mom and me that "this call is my New Years gift to you" and went on to tell us the good news: the samples were negative for cancer.

My, oh my! Deep breaths and a sigh of relief as a smile returned to my face.

With this scare behind us and three more months ahead of us, this may have been a New Years gift, but we still had work to do!

Happy New Year, my little girl!

CHAPTER 19

MAN'S BEST FRIEND

In 1995 I stepped carefully into retirement. I was tired. I'd done everything I'd ever dreamed of doing, traveled to places I had never dreamed of visiting, and racked up several million frequent flyer miles, some of which I haven't used. Several years later, I decided to take Social Security early. Now I was officially retired!

Looking back, all of this seems like a dream that took place yesterday. Retiring early was probably the biggest gamble of my life. I talked it over with Mom and we agreed that if we were careful, really careful, our savings might just last until it was time for us to depart this world.

A couple of other things happened during my retirement. I never expected to add a dog to our slowly declining family of retired show cats, but we did, thanks to an uninvited guest. As you know by now, that was your sister Sabrina, your guardian angel. Suddenly I found that owning a dog required adjusting my schedule to fit her amazing memory. Like you, your sister never missed a meal, a carrot, or a treat when they were due.

During her time with us, nearly eleven years, she generated enough surgical revenue to help reduce the national debt. Just kidding, Sabrina! She also demonstrated through nonstop love and devotion why the expression "man's best friend" must have been coined.

Then you came along, my love. Sabrina's medical needs taught Mom and me the importance of pet medical insurance, so we signed up, hoping never to have to use it.

Four years passed and then, in a period of eight days, we were glad we had it. A simple surgical procedure scared us out of our minds. Cancer! You had cancer, and it was inoperable. We were told you were probably going to die. Yet, here we are. The thought that I still might lose you hangs over us, and for some unknown reason I am reminded of the phrase "man's best friend."

If it hadn't been for a gentle giant named Lokey there might never have been a Sabrina, Tia, or Holly in my life.

Sabrina epitomized "man's best friend," and when you joined our family, you assumed the mantle and have worn it with dignity.

Sabrina never had a cat sister to know and love. She tried. Believe me she tried, but our finicky felines would have no part of it.

Holly is my best friend and she's a...

Excuse me, you thought Holly was just a small dog? Sorry to disappoint you, but your best bud is definitely a cat, an Ocicat.

Is Holly man's best friend too?

No, that distinction belongs to you, but you are *her* best friend.

I know.

The other night, Mom said to me, "Do you think Tia is aging fast?"

Who, me? Old? You've got to be kidding!

Sadly, I had to agree. Maybe cancer and months of chemotherapy is causing your muzzle to turn white, and as much as I hate to admit it, at times you do seem to be slowing down a step or two at the end of the day. We'll have to ask Dr. Ward about your muzzle when we take you for your next chemotherapy injection. Maybe you need an extra nap or two during the day.

Tia, life is a collage of experiences. I know you don't understand what that means, but just imagine seeing lots and lots of pictures of our time together, all at once.

Some people call themselves dog and cat "owners." Not us. We've never "owned" any of you. *Loved* you, yes— for as long as possible, but *owned*? Never!

No matter what I do to you, or forget to do for you, you are always there for me. You ask so little and yet you never stop giving.

The other day after taking your afternoon walk and receiving a carrot treat for a job well done, you put on quite a show for someone who has been living on borrowed time. Watching your antics was hard to believe. You finished a treat, washed it down with an ice cube, and suddenly began galloping around the house. Faster and faster you ran as you kept making the loop from the living room down the hall, through the kitchen, into the dining room, and back to the living room. After several circumnavigations you flew out of the kitchen and landed with a thud, on your belly, in your dog bed.

Once you realized you were there, you stood up, shook yourself violently, then buried your muzzle in your bed and growled ferociously as you pretended to clean it. Satisfied that you had completed the first act of your show, you flipped over on your back and began spinning around, with your legs flailing in the air as if you were running, but going nowhere. It was very unladylike!

Once you completed this exhibition you rolled over on your stomach, sprang to your feet, leapt in the air and made one more round of the house before ending back in your bed, on your side, looking at me to see if I had been watching.

Old, schmold! Let's see you or Mom do that!

I couldn't even if I wanted too. Just remember what the doctors said...

I know!

Sick?

Dying?

Dead?

Not my little girl!

Will Rogers got it right when he said, "If there are no dogs in heaven, then when I die I want to go where they went."

Tia, you are not only "man's best friend" you have always been the funniest, most lovable show in town.

That expression has been around forever, and during a moment of reflection, I did a little searching to find out how it came about. Would you believe me if I told you a lawyer coined it?

Once I read the story behind the phrase, it changed my thinking about lawyers, and when people read this short story it will probably change the way many of them look at the legal fraternity as well. But speaking for myself...

I think it was coined just for Sabrina and you.

Gentlemen of the Jury

The phrase "Man's Best Friend" originated in a court of law. On October 28, 1869, a man's dog (named "Old Drum") was shot to death by a neighbor. Animals had no rights back in those days, but the man wanted justice so he hired 3 lawyers to sue the man who shot his dog. One of the lawyers, George Graham Vest, originally came up with the phrase "Man's Best Friend" during his final summation to the jury. By the time he was finished with his speech the jury only took 2 minutes to reach a verdict. The jury awarded the victim $5 (a very large sum back then). The jury wanted the man to be sent to prison, but there were no laws governing this type of incident so the judge was not able to honor the jury's request.

This is a record of the summation of the lawyer.

The best friend a man has in this world may turn against him and become his enemy. His son and daughter that he has reared with loving care may become ungrateful. Those who are nearest and dearest to us, those whom we trust with our happiness and our good name, may become traitors to their faith. The money that a man has, he may lose. It flies away from him when he may need it the most. Man's reputation may be sacrificed in a moment of ill-considered action. The people who are prone to fall on their knees and do us honor when success is with us may be the first to throw the stone of malice when failure settles its cloud upon our head. The only absolutely unselfish friend a man may have in this selfish world, the one that never deserts him, the one that never proves ungrateful or treacherous, is his dog.

A man's dog stands by him in prosperity and poverty, in health and sickness. He will sleep on the cold ground when the wintry winds blow and the snow drives fiercely, if only he can be near his master's side. He will kiss the hand that has no food to offer, he will lick the wounds and sores that come and encounter with the roughness of the world. He guards the sleep of a pauper as if he were a prince. When all other friends desert...he remains.

When riches take wings and reputations fall to pieces, he is as constant in his love as the sun in its journey through the heavens. If fortune drives the master forth, an outcast into the world friendless and homeless, the faithful dog asks no higher privilege then that of accompanying him, to guard him against danger, to fight against his enemies, and when the last scene of all comes, and death takes his master in its embrace and his body is laid away in the cold ground, no matter if all other friends pursue their way, there by his graveside will the noble dog be found, his head between his paws and his eyes sad, but open in alert watchfulness, faithful and true even to death.

From Heart of Ohio Boxer Rescue

Tia, we've come a long way together, on a journey that I wish would never end, but for now, let's focus upon your sixth birthday in March and, of course, when you reach full remission in April. Remember what I told you when we started this journey:

Yesterday is gone,
tomorrow is not here,

so make the most of each today!

Month after month I have watched you do just that as you come bounding out of your kennel in the morning, tail wagging as you head for the kitchen looking for someone to kiss. You, my little girl, are one big, happy-go-lucky adult child. No matter how much I may have been worried at times, your amazing spirit has lifted me up—when I should have been the one doing the heavy lifting.

These past twenty-one months have consisted of exhilarating highs and lows that others cannot comprehend unless they have traveled the same road. Yet, your disposition has never changed, and that's why I know that no matter what life throws at you, you will brush it aside, tear through the day, and leap into your kennel at night as if nothing in your life has changed.

You are my strength!

When you came into our lives nearly six years ago we saw you as a fearful little ball of fur hoping that these strangers would care for and protect you the way your mother had done.

You didn't know it at the time, but we needed each other!

It didn't take long for you to fill the hole in our hearts that was left when Sabrina was called home.

As I look back at our time together I can state with assurance that you and Sabrina are living proof that the phrase "man's best friend" is being carried with dignity. You are both more than Mom and I ever expected.

To this day, you continue to be the silly little girl that lights up our life with your antics.

Thank you Lokey, we will never forget you!

CHAPTER 20

NIGHT-NIGHT

"T..."

Dad...
"Time to go to sleep. Love you."
What's love?
"It's a very special feeling, very delicate. Sometimes you don't recognize it until you are faced with the possibility of losing it!"
You love me!
"And don't you forget it. Every night, and especially these past twenty-one months, before I go to sleep I close my eyes and tell Mom how much I love her and to sleep well.

"Then, I talk with Sabrina. I ask her to watch over our extended family in heaven and to ask Tony, Charlie, Wolfe, Randy, and Rachel, and Granny and Grampy Landy and Wowk, to send their love, strength, and determination to your little sister Holly. She's Sabrina's surrogate."
What's a surrogate?
"A friend and helper, a bridge between heaven and us."

Then do you go to sleep?

"No. My night's not complete until I remind Sabrina to wrap her paws around you, hold you tight, and transfer her amazing strength and love directly to you."

So that's what I've been feeling when you tell me to have good doggie dreams?"

"She and I are the last ones to send you love every night."

I'm really lucky to have so many helpers watching over me!

"That's what love is all about. Night-night!"

CHAPTER 21
HELPFUL HINTS AND LAST THOUGHTS

Tia's story has afforded me an opportunity to discuss a subject that will walk with me every day of my life: the pain of losing loved ones and the fight to save our amazing children. We may not have been able to save all of them, but we never stopped trying.

Life is a learning experience. That's why I want to share a few thoughts with you that may help you when considering a four-legged friend, and before it is time for your child to take its last walk across the Rainbow Bridge.

There are a number of books and articles that deal with selecting a pet child, grief, grieving, and understanding the loss of a canine or feline friend.

My comments, like Tia's story, are not written by an expert, just someone that has been where you may be about to go.

As you read and think about the next few pages I hope this summary helps you to explore your feelings and decisions. Chances are you will add a few thoughts of your own to this list or create a new list that expresses your experiences and that you can "pay forward."

Thinking about bringing a four-legged child into your life? Don't be fooled by that lovable look or that sad face staring up at you. There is more to bringing a pet child into your life then that warm, tingly feeling you are experiencing.

You aren't just bringing a pet into your life, you are adding a new family member, so be sure that you are willing to stay the course before you sail off together.

This may be a lot to grasp in one gulp, but think about all the strays you see running around. Chances are they were taken in by someone just like you, with all of the best intentions until—well, you can place your own ending on this one.

Ever heard it said that "a pet is a forever friend?" Make sure you allow the word *forever* time to sink in.

Read and then think about the breed and the size of pet you intend to bring into your life. Big dog, small dog, or one in between? Size is an important consideration. I know you've probably seen or read stories about people who share a one-bedroom apartment with a St. Bernard, but really! The thought may bring a smile to your face and remind you of the little car in the circus with twelve clowns inside, but is that really fair to the dog?

Of course not! Everyone needs a little space he can call his own.

Equally important, will your planned guest be several times the size of your children? And how will that particular breed, or mix of breeds, interact with youngsters who like to pull, tug, and poke?

Think about what you will need at hand on day one of the rest of your life with a canine or feline friend. Read, think, and make lists.

Food, toys and a place your pet can call its own, work for both kittens and pups. Kittens will need a litter box and kitty litter. Pups need collars and leashes. A "how-to" manual and publications dealing with kittens and pups—and in the case of pedigreed pups, books that deal specifically with your particular breed—are worth the investment even before you begin your search for a pet child.

Of equal importance, have a vet in mind before you get started.

Your four-legged friend has needs. Take the time to read and plan ahead as best you can. There will always be something you forgot, but thinking ahead will get both of you off on the right foot.

Where to find your new family member. Your local humane society is a great place to start. Your local newspaper can often steer you toward a new litter of kittens or puppies and an opportunity to meet the mother and possibly the father.

Looking for a pedigreed pup or kitten. Not everyone can, but if you have the financial means and are thinking about a pedigreed pup or kitten look up the American Kennel Club for dogs or the Cat Fanciers' Association for cats. These national bodies can direct you to breeders within a reasonable distance of your home. You will find that these breeders love their children—all of them—just as much as you will. This love and professionalism helps to create wonderful pet children.

Meet the Parents. If you are working with a professional breeder take the time to meet the parents of your prospective puppy. If Mom and Dad are gentle and full of love, chances are their offspring will be as well.

Ask the breeder to allow you to meet your potential family member when it is six or seven weeks old. Wait at least nine weeks before you separate the pup or kitten of your choice from his mom and littermates. Check your state's regulations to see what shots and special care should have been provided by the seller.

Don't be bashful. Get down on the floor or on the grass and interact with the little tykes. Making a choice is not as easy as some make it out to be. If one pup attracts your attention and has not been taken, ask the breeder to place a colored ribbon or some form of identification on your pet child so that when it is time to bring him home you will know that he is "the one."

Thinking about an older dog or cat? Your local humane society is a good place to start.

If you are looking for a specific breed of dog, check to see if there is a breed rescue in your area or talk with well-respected dog trainers and your proposed vet. Both can often turn you on to an older dog or cat that is well-grounded and in need of a loving family.

Training. It may be love at first sight, but take my word for it, love begins when the training ends.

National pet supply chains offer basic training and socialization skills, but don't be surprised if your little charger forgets everything he learned five minutes after you finish your last class.

If you discover you need more help, check out trainers in your area and talk with several of their references. If they train in a class setting, make time to watch a few lessons to see how dogs interact and respond to training.

For bigger dogs, you may want to talk to your professional breeder about a trainer, consult your local police department, or look for training sites that specialize in police/drug and other unique training. Chances are they also provide obedience training.

The key to success is not just the trainer. Winning the battle for leadership requires practice, practice, and more practice!

Picking a vet. This requires more than just reaching for the Yellow Pages. You may have to kick a few tires before you find the right one, but believe me it is worth the effort.

You want a vet who listens to your perceived problem, responds in a language that you can understand, spends what you feel is a reasonable amount of time with your pet child, handles your child with love and care, is willing to tell you when he or she doesn't know the answer to your problem, and is able to refer you on to a specialist. When it comes to pills, is your vet willing to write prescriptions for those drugs that you can buy at your local pharmacy for a fraction of the cost of purchasing the same pill from the veterinary clinic?

If you pick a veterinarian and soon find you have made a mistake, don't be afraid to make a change. It took us three vets before we felt comfortable with our choice, but getting it right is important for you and your pet.

Thought about pet insurance? You may never need it, but when you do and you don't have it, you will wish you did. Visit the Internet and check out the various pet insurance programs that are available for dogs and cats.

Talk to your veterinarian about pet insurance. Chances are you can find one that fits your budget and delivers what it promises.

Don't play God. Having that special child with you for a few extra days, weeks, or months may forestall the inevitable, but think about what you are putting the pet through.

Would you want to live this way?

Consider your options in a crisis. As you have learned from reading Tia's story, sometimes it is wise to step back and, in a moment of silence, trust your instincts.

When we were told that Tia had little chance of survival, as horrific as that sounded there was time for us to try and save her before the cancer spread and pain ensued.

On the other hand, when Sabrina's cancer was discovered, we knew that a loving end was far better than a few months of torture as we watched her slowly and painfully slip away.

We have always reached out to secure the best medical support available. If Tia's treatment had not shown positive signs, we would never have allowed her to live in pain.

The decision to end a life is difficult and painful, but sometimes it is the most loving thing you can do.

Thanks for the memories! The love of your life, that canine or feline friend that has loved you without preconditions for oh so many years, deserves the dignity of early retirement rather than a painful end of life.

Don't get me wrong, I'm not suggesting you set a date for a departure, only that when your child begins to lose her sight, and hearing, and needs to be carried outside to perform bodily functions, sometimes one last walk together is the best solution. It allows both of you to remember the good times you shared and sends your special friend to a wonderful new life.

Be with them at the end. Nothing says "I love you" more than being with your loved ones when it is time for them to be placed in God's hands.

Over the years we have always made it a point to be "hands on." This has been our way of letting our pet child know and feel how much he or she has meant to us.

Don't be afraid to shed a tear. That fur ball that came into your life asking only love and protection has touched you in ways you will never know until it is time to return it.

Don't be surprised or ashamed to show your emotions. The longer you keep them hidden, the greater the pain. I know!

Little things mean a lot. I have a number of pictures and mementos that remind me of my favorite cat and dog children, but the one closest to my heart is a silver dog bone I wear on a silver chain around my neck. It contains some of Sabrina's ashes and will one day be joined by another bone.

But Tia, my beautiful little child, there is no need to hurry!

Down in the dumps (aka depressed)? Spend some quiet time writing down all of the ways your child touched you and what it meant to you.

Don't like to write? Then sit back, close your eyes, and spend a quiet moment with your thoughts. You will be surprised how much remembering helps to reduce your pain.

Share your thoughts with your spouse, significant other, or friends. This may be difficult, but take a few deep breaths and share—you will be amazed how much releasing your feelings helps. Do it sooner rather than later; the longer you wait the more difficult it becomes.

Don't let friends or family get you down. Some people will never understand the bond that exists between you and your pet child. You are not wrong; *they* are—for doubting you.

Still down in the dumps? Help is nearby! Your church, local hospice chapter or pet loss support lines are excellent resources when you need an outlet through which to share your feelings. Some work one-on-one, others use a group format that affords you an opportunity to share your feelings with others who understand and/or are experiencing the same pain.

Give yourself time to acknowledge and understand and heal the pain of loss before bringing another pet child into your life.

Google and other search engines can help you to find a support system.

Should I bring the same breed into my life? This may sound like a broken record, but follow your heart. Should you choose the same breed? If you do, don't be surprised if, no matter how hard you try, you find yourself comparing your new child to the one you lost. It is only natural.

When is the right time? The best advice Mitch gave us was, "Listen to your heart and your eyes, they will steer you in the right direction!"

I hope this summary is helpful. Given time, your canine or feline family member will create a place in your heart that will make the experience of parenting all the more amazing and when the time comes to take that last walk a part of you will never be the same again, but that's a good thing because...

There is no pain greater than the loss of a special friend.

Love has no time limit—love is forever!

If you would like to know how Tia is doing, e-mail me at: nodl2938@comcast.net subject "Tia".